- **Little Laureates Vol I**
Edited by Claire Tupholme

First published in Great Britain in 2006 by:
Young Writers
Remus House
Coltsfoot Drive
Peterborough
PE2 9JX
Telephone: 01733 890066
Website: www.youngwriters.co.uk

All Rights Reserved

© *Copyright Contributors 2006*

SB ISBN 1 84602 384 X

Foreword

Young Writers was established in 1991 and has been passionately devoted to the promotion of reading and writing in children and young adults ever since. The quest continues today. Young Writers remains as committed to the fostering of burgeoning poetic and literary talent as ever.

This year's Young Writers competition has proven as vibrant and dynamic as ever and we are delighted to present a showcase of the best poetry from across the UK. Each poem has been carefully selected from a wealth of *Playground Poets* entries before ultimately being published in this, our thirteenth primary school poetry series.

Once again, we have been supremely impressed by the overall high quality of the entries we have received. The imagination, energy and creativity which has gone into each young writer's entry made choosing the best poems a challenging and often difficult but ultimately hugely rewarding task - the general high standard of the work submitted amply vindicating this opportunity to bring their poetry to a larger appreciative audience.

We sincerely hope you are pleased with our final selection and that you will enjoy *Playground Poets - Little Laureates Vol I* for many years to come.

Contents

Prisca Gusha (11)   1

All Saints' CE (VC) Primary School, Maldon
Bronté Culleton (10)   1
Liam Xavier (10)   2
William Mortimer (11)   2
Lindsey Richards (10)   2
Nicholas Sparkes (9)   3
Rachel Docherty (9)   3

Ardstraw Primary School, Ardstraw
Jill Hamilton (9)   3
Sophia McGonigle (9)   4

Ashleigh Primary School, Barnstaple
Lewis Delphin (10)   4

Barker's Lane Community School, Wrexham
Rachel Jarvis (11)   5
Morgan Jones (10)   5
Stephanie Bellis (10)   6
Rhian Davies (10)   7
Luke Davies (10)   8
Jason Daniels (10)   9
Sophie Davies (10)   10
Ruth Cowlishaw (10)   10

Beacon Primary School, Willenhall
Grace Wilkinson (9)   11
Jack Williams (11)   11
Corey Reeves (10)   12
Rebecca Murphy (10)   12
Adam Walton (11)   13
Kieran Kendall (10)   13
Adam Hampton (9)   13
Terri-Leigh Sargeant (9)   14

Saul Rayner (10)	14
Nicole Painter (9)	15
Matthew Wilcox (9)	15
Ben Bates (10)	16
Kayleigh Webster (9)	16
Abbie Myles (9)	16
Natalie Stewart (10)	17
Ashley Maiden (9)	17
Jessica Whitehouse (9)	18
Rachel Grant (10)	18
Stevie Knowles (11)	19
Adam Parsons (10)	19
Lauren Harris (11)	20
Jade Woolams (10)	20
Aaron Chew (10)	21
Arron Bates (10)	21
Leigh Etheridge (10)	22
Alleigha Evans (10)	23
Lee Dougliss (11)	23
Joshua Bowker (10)	24
Lauren Deeming (10)	24
Bonnie Tsim (10)	25
Connor Lockley (11)	25
Samuel Dewsbery (9)	26
Emily Nicholls (10)	26
Ellis Brookes (10)	27
Zowie Rook (10)	27
Nathaniel Holland-Bright (11)	28
Callum Roberts (9)	28
Liam Craig Allen (9)	29
Summer May Higgins (10)	30
Nathan Mann (10)	31
Jordan Gary Hall (11)	31
Rheanne Griffiths (10)	32
Charlotte Corbett (9)	32
Jamie Francis (10)	33
Aaron Parry-Percox (10)	34
Sabrina Wolverson (11)	35

Bede Burn Primary School, Jarrow
Jessica Birch (8)	35
Jennifer Parkins (10)	36
Dale Brown (10)	36
Richard Dennis (10)	37
Nicholas Pallister (9)	37
Josie Miller (11)	38
Matthew Wood (10)	38
Jack Davies (11)	39
Kieran Day (10)	39
Ethan Nichol (9)	40
Fred Davies (9)	40
Abbie Collis (9)	40
Lewis Crooks (10)	41

Belle Vue Primary School, Stourbridge
Elliot Bridgewater (10)	41
Harry Thynne (10)	42
Hannah Potter (11)	43
Charly Willder (10)	43
Bethan Nutting (10)	44
Luke Rowley (10)	44
Charlotte Skelding (10)	45
Sally Ovenall	45

Bricknell Primary School, Kingston upon Hull
Daniel Phillips (9)	46
Ryan Hirons (9)	46
Matthew McDougall (9)	46
Jacob Green (10)	46
Sam Robinson (10)	47
Isobelle Anderson (9)	47
Calum Hart (9)	47
Charlotte Hines (9)	47
Louis West (9)	48
India Robinson (9)	48
Jason Young (9)	48
Charlotte Pickering (9)	48
Lewis Turner (9)	49
Sophie Chapman (9)	49

Dan Jones (9)	49
Amelia Wickenden (9)	49
Natalie Bayley (9)	50
Emily Walker (9)	50
Francesca Medcalf (10)	50
Alex Donnelly (9)	50
Rachel Innes (10)	51
Maya Singleton (9)	51
Dominic Slater (10)	51
James Wilson (9)	51

Brooke Primary School, Norwich

Theo Robson (10)	52
Joseph Bonner (10)	52
Amy Gilks (10)	53
George Saville (9)	53
Helena Thomas (10)	54
Isobel Shaw Pritchard (9)	54
Alice Martin (11)	55
Jessica Stanton (10)	55
Jenny Hill (9)	56
Katy Leeson (9)	56
Julia Duncan (9)	57
Alexander Jane (9)	57
Tortie Ward (10)	58
Hollie Campbell (10)	59
Jessica Taylor (9)	59
Ellie Absalom (9)	60
Matthew Boyle (9)	60
Rebecca Burrage (10)	61
Daniel Earl (10)	61
Rosie Swain (10)	62
Jacob Clarry (10)	62
Cameron Clarke (9)	63
Jessica Harmer (10)	63
Mark Lawes (11)	64
Ben Mitchell (9)	64

Brookside Junior School, Romford
    Alannah Sinnott   65
    Abbie Tindall   65
    Danielle Downham   66
    Courtney Jones   66

Buckstone Primary School, Edinburgh
    Thomas Bartos (9)   67

Buick Memorial Primary School, Cullybackey
    Amy Galbraith (9)   68
    Adam Greer (9)   68
    Natalie Swann (9)   69
    Bethany Coulter (9)   69
    Charles Orr (9)   70
    Matthew Beattie (10)   70
    Luke Henry (9)   71
    Gemma McClenaghan (9)   71
    Michael McKelvey (10)   72
    Daniel Bestek (9)   72
    Chloe McAleese (9)   73
    Ellen Dunlop (8)   73
    Nicola Anderson (8)   74
    Janessa Morgan (8)   74
    Georgina Shaw (8)   75
    Luke Simpson (9)   75
    Timothy Spence (9)   76
    Craig Coates (9)   76
    Rhianna Campbell (8)   77
    Robbie Campbell (9)   77
    Ben Gaston (8)   78
    Alana Duff (8)   79
    Nicole Paul (9)   80
    Bryony McCleery (9)   80
    Lauren Perry (9)   81
    Stuart Wylie (8)   81
    Jessica Reid (10)   82
    Jordan Campbell (9)   82
    Kurtis Given (9)   83
    Charlotte Carney (9)   83

Megan Rea (10)	84
Reuben Lamont (10)	84
Matthew McCallion (9)	85
Robbie Moore (9)	85
Thomas Mellon (9)	86

Burray School, Orkney

Elyse Miller (11)	86
Cheryl Smith (11)	87
Stefan Taylor (11)	87
Claire Corsie (11)	88
Ethan Prior-Sanderson (11)	88
Grace Corsie (9)	89
Erin Smith (9)	89
David Sinclair (9)	90
Ruairidh Gough (9)	90
Connor Malloy (11)	91
Shannon Hume (11)	91
Lily Humphreys (10)	92

Canon Maggs CE Junior School, Bedworth

Matthew Broadhurst (9)	92
Georgia Snaith (9)	93
Christopher Snaith (9)	93
Bethany Draper (9)	94
Shannon Reade (9)	94
Paige Johnson (9)	95
Amy Brown (9)	95
Katie Molesworth (9)	96
Jacob Morson (9)	96
Pagan Conroy (9)	97
Joshua Bagnall (9)	97
Daniel Day (10)	98
Lewis Herdman (10)	98
Chloe Smith (9)	99
Charlotte Mallabone (9)	99
Connor Goold (9)	100
Ryan Allsopp (9)	100
Amie Johnson (9)	101
Daniel Cunnington (9)	101
Shevonne Broadbent (9)	102

Rachel Grant (9)	102
Toni Lovell (9)	103
Olivia Fitz-James Johnson (9)	103
Loic Wan (9)	104
Laura Collins (9)	104
Katie-Ann Northall (9)	105
Niall MacCallum (9)	105
Joshua Loughrey (9)	106

Cathedral Primary School, Motherwell

Shaun Donnelly (11)	106
Lauren Thorburn (11)	107
Fiona Ross (11)	107
Shaun Nicholls (11)	108
Jordan Lewis (11)	109
Adrian Pollock (11)	109
Jack Mullen (11)	110
Jodi Clinton (11)	110
Lauren Bolton (11)	111
Emma Young (11)	111
Emmanuel Ndlovu (11)	112
Lauren McShannon (11)	112
Robyn Delaney (11)	113
Adele Buchanan (11)	113
Erin Eadie (11)	114
Allan Hopkinson (11)	115
Michael McCabe (11)	115
Natalie Thomson (11)	116
Megan Cook (11)	116
Katie Cunningham (11)	117
Anthony Maguire (10)	117
Lucy McCarron (11)	118
Lauren Carroll (10)	118
Nicole Leggate (11)	119
Rachel Shields (10)	119
Rachel McCann (10)	120
Mhairi Duncan (11)	121
Colette Carr (10)	121
Aimee Flanagan (10)	122
Lauren McKinnon (10)	122
Kerry McDade (11)	123

Rachael Lamarra (10)	123
Chloe Ruiz (10)	124
Stefan Ward (10)	124
Jessica O'Brien (10)	125
Louise Murray (11)	125
Paul McGill (10)	126
Rebecca Fitzsimmons (10)	127
Amy Stark (10)	128
Jordan Crisp (11)	129

Charley Memorial Primary School, Belfast

Andrew Davis (11)	129
Ami Thompson (10)	130
Emma Thompson (10)	131
Anne Henderson (9)	132
Christopher Cullen (10)	132
Adam Gorringe (8)	133

Coed Glas Primary School, Llanishen

Lauren Galliford (8)	133
Ryan Moore (8)	134
Meg Owen (8)	134
Natalie Vaughan (10)	135
Charlea Heathfield-Eades (8)	135
Bethan John (8)	136
George Davies (8)	136
Steffan Hugh Davies (9)	136
William Mesoud (8)	137
Mawgan Newman (8)	137
Lewis Prole (8)	137
Freya Cuthbert (8)	138
Kirsty Williams (8)	138
Laura Mulder (8)	138
Joseph Price (8)	139
Taylor Brown (8)	139
Joanne Chandler (8)	139
Brendan Kearon (10)	140
Celyn Keene-Proctor (8)	140
Molly Proudman (11)	140
Bethan Jenkins (10)	141
Danielle Thwaites (10)	141

Lauren Hyde (11)	142
George Carson (9)	142
Jessica Dyer (10)	143
Kia Shah (8)	143
Sian Ellis (10)	144
Sophie Rooke (11)	144
Christine Grimes (10)	145
Jessica Williams (11)	145
Daniel Bardsley (10)	146
Morgan Church (11)	146
Megan Chisholm-Jones (10)	147
Nicole Hicks (10)	147
Thomas Pine (10)	148
Daryl Mackay (8)	148
Sophia Ouaaziz (10)	149
Danielle O'Brien (10)	149
Natalie Lloyd-Gale (8)	150
Kirsty O'Donnell (10)	150
Jodie Welsh (10)	151
Katie Nash (11)	151
Jaimie-Lee O'Shea (11)	151
Sophie Wall (8)	152
Angharad Brown (8)	152
Samuel Tuson (11)	152
Sophie Eddy (10)	153
Ashleigh Williams (10)	153
Josie Dunne (10)	153
Annalise Daly (10)	154
Georgina Mathlin (10)	154
Daniel Heathfield-Eades (11)	154
Hannah Jowett (10)	155
Josh Woods (10)	155
Emily Jones (11)	155

Culloden Primary School, London

Taslima Akther (9)	156
Imran Hussain (10)	156
Dalena Dang (9)	157
Ajwad Ahmed (9)	157
Randa Hassan (9)	158
Soumayah Chakir (9)	159

Valerie Bensalem (9)	159
Tanjima Khanam (9)	160
Jamal Uddin (9)	160
Shipu Alom (9)	161
Sahidah Shahrazad (10)	161
Chantelle da Silva (9)	162
Tofayel Ahmad Choudrey (9)	162
Connor Smith (9)	162

Darvel Primary School, Darvel

Jacqueline Baker (11)	163
Erin Provan (10)	163
James Watt (11)	164
Jennifer Paterson (11)	164
Sorcha Johnstone (11)	165
Alice Boyd (10)	165
Devlin Greig (11)	166
Sarah Murray (11)	166
Andrew Hyslop (11)	167
Scott Elder (11)	167
Sean Hunter (11)	168
Gemma Yeudall (11)	168

Eastbury Farm JMI & Nursery School, Northwood

Isabella Kowalski (9)	169
Becky Tolliday (10)	169
Lauren Slater (9)	170
Kieran Morrison (10)	170
Stephanie Challis (9)	171
Ellie Weston (10)	171
Kate Miller (11)	172
Alexander Butcher (10)	172
Phebe Brown (11)	173
Adam Gibbor (9)	173
James Nicholas (9)	174
Christine Swain (11)	174
Katherine Barraclough (9)	175
Rachel Sibson (10)	175
Chloe Davies (9)	176
James Price (9)	176
Hayley Graham (9)	176

Hannah Stephens (11)	177
Tessa Clark (10)	177
Amy Decker (9)	178
Kitty Corbett (9)	178
Thirza McDonald (11)	179
Sachin Dholakia (10)	179
Matthew Chong (9)	180
Jake Thomas (11)	180
Molly Welton (9)	180
Reece Thomas (9)	181
David Braham (10)	181
Harry Lock (10)	182
Charlie Millard (9)	182
James Hayes (9)	182
Harry Millard (10)	183
Stuart Patrick (10)	183
Franceska Gudiens (10)	184
Ryan Kirkman (9)	184
Sarah Mattson (11)	185
Ali-Reza Daya (10)	185
Abbie Neale	186
Brennan Cleveland (10)	186
Katie Allday (9)	187
Karis Parfitt (10)	187
Steff Capittelli (10)	188
Lucy Miah (9)	188
Georgia Barton (10)	189
Kourosh Khodabakhsh (9)	189
Charlotte McDonagh (10)	190
Sophie Williams (10)	190
Mia Zambakides (10)	191
Evie Gardiner (9)	191
Lauren Smith (10)	192
Katherine Head (10)	192
Charlotte Bignall (10)	193
Lauren Hatton (10)	193
Sameera Hamid (11)	194
Sam Southwell (10)	194
Charlotte Melinek (10)	195

Garlinge Junior School, Margate

Samuel Castle (7)	195
Abbey Golder (8)	196
Charley Jackson-Powell (7)	196
Rebecca Mann (8)	197
Holly Hill (8)	197
Jemma Eccott (8)	198
Dexter Hamilton (8)	198
Louise Cannon (8)	199
Ben Sheppard (7)	199
Courtney Clarke (8)	200
Jessica Voss (7)	200
Laura Robertshaw (8)	201
Kieran Doyle (8)	201
Aidan Hepworth (7)	202
Harriet Chapman (8)	202
Lauren Hart (8)	203
Charne Welch (8)	203
Simon Boyd (8)	204
Amy Mallett (10)	204
Erustus Agutu (8)	205
Aimee Chamberlain (7)	205
India Toomey (9)	206
Chloe Roberts (8)	206
Elizabeth Randall (9)	207

Gladstone Primary School, Barry

Tom Webb (10)	207
Hannah James (10)	208
Sophie Owens (11)	208
Amy James (10)	209
Ritchie Aspinall	209
James Cassam (10)	209
Carrianne Rogers (10)	210
Connor Rowlands	210
Jacques Sloman (10)	211
Ellie Goldsby	211
Ryan Jones (10)	211
Jannat Ahmed (10)	212
Lucy Dimond (10)	212
Georgia Graham (10)	213

Rhia Dutton (10)	213
Chaliese Anderson-Ludvigsen (10)	214
Franklin Roe (11)	214
Chantelle Selby	215
Jessica Lant	215
Jade Rees	216
Kelly Alford (10)	216
Elliott Clissold (11)	217
Elise Tyler	217
Carrie Aspinall	218
Charlotte Mills	218
Sam Williams (10)	219
Sam Hillier (10)	219
Nathan Richards (11)	219
Ffion McCullough (10)	220
Sophie McCabe	220

Hayshead Primary School, Arbroath

Rhian Gall (11)	221
Michael Willmott (11)	222
Caitlin Grant (11)	223
Sophie Willmott (11)	224
Denise Buchan (11)	225
Russell Henderson (11)	226
Gavin Cook (11)	227
Lee Smith (11)	227
Dean Smith (11)	228
Shelby Green (10)	228
Natasha Herald (11)	229
Hannah Harris (11)	229
Terri McKenzie (11)	229
Daniel Campbell (11)	230
Reese Maison (10)	230
Kyle McIntosh (11)	230
Jay Millar (11)	231
Sean Muir (11)	231
Cameron Ramage (11)	231
Daniel Simpson (10)	232
John Ryan (10)	232
Jason Wood (11)	233
Shannon Sinclair (11)	233

Paige Findlay (11)	234
Liam Smith (11)	234
John Taylor (11)	235
David Teviotdale (12)	235
Stephanie Ward (10)	236
John Woodcock (11)	236
Luke Waddilove (11)	236
Jamie Elliott (10)	237
Liam Winton (11)	238
Lori Cargill (11)	238

Ysgol Gynradd Bronington, Whitchurch

Rachel Mottershead (9)	238
Abigail Fawcett, Heather Davies & Ellie Ryder (10)	239
Richard Jones (10)	239
Sam Evans (10) & Michael Roberts	240
Jacob Kendall (9)	240
Bethany Loveridge (11) & Joshua Bailey (10)	241
Sammy O'Brien (9)	241

The Poems

Terrible Tricks

Imagine you see a person holding his head
Blood dripping to the floor
All you see is a neck but *no* head
Try and touch the neck but don't get too close
Don't

Imagine you see a hand
With no fingernail
It will be moving on its own
But don't you dare touch
It might grab your hand and you will get covered in blood

Imagine you see a ghost
What do you do?
I will probably run away
This ghost will not be scared
But you will be!

Prisca Gusha (11)

Bloody Mary

B lack-hearted Mary, queen of darkness
L ucky people never saw her axe's sharpness
O nly Catholics had this honour
O nly Protestants became head donors
D idn't waste time on starting to slaughter
Y ou know if she had one she would have killed her own daughter.

M urder by name, murder by nature
A t the end she will come and get you
R un for your life
Y ou will save yourself a lot of strife.

Bronté Culleton (10)
All Saints' CE (VC) Primary School, Maldon

The Wolf

He with the sleek, black nose,
At night to the forest to hunt he goes.
He is nocturnal
So every morning he has a doze.
In the dark night he lurks to kill deer,
With his chocolate-brown eyes he peers
But the terrible poachers he fears.

Liam Xavier (10)
All Saints' CE (VC) Primary School, Maldon

The Serpent

In woodland realms at night all you can see,
Are two emerald diamonds as plain as can be,
On pitch-black nights he moves through crinkled leaves.
With never a friend he slithers along the dusty track,
And then he bites you in the back,
For he is the lord of serpents black.

William Mortimer (11)
All Saints' CE (VC) Primary School, Maldon

The Whale

He swims all day in the azure sea,
Catching krill swiftly,
He can dive down deep but carefully,
He has baleen for his teeth,
Looking with soft and gentle eyes in the coral reef,
Of all the whales he is the chief.

Lindsey Richards (10)
All Saints' CE (VC) Primary School, Maldon

The Snake

Slithers along the mountain high,
He feels as if he's slithering in the sky,
He sees the birds fly by,
He sees his prey and jumps out,
Living in the mountain,
Doesn't live on trout,
He finds a hog with a giant snout.

Nicholas Sparkes (9)
All Saints' CE (VC) Primary School, Maldon

The Turtle

She swims in the silent seas,
Making all the other fish freeze,
Then the small angelfish flees.
Looking around the weed,
She looks at sharks with tons of greed,
And finds a settlement to feast and feed.

Rachel Docherty (9)
All Saints' CE (VC) Primary School, Maldon

My . . . ?

When I walk I see a figure
Tall and black and getting bigger.
I start to think, *what can it be?*
And then it starts to follow me.
When I get home to my mum,
She says, 'Jill, you look so worried. Are you ill?'

Then she explains, 'Don't worry, dear,
Or have a fright.
It only happens with sun and light.'
My shadow!

Jill Hamilton (9)
Ardstraw Primary School, Ardstraw

Fruit Custard

Fruit custard so slimy and runny
It runs down your throat
And into your tummy.
It has flavours like apples,
Bananas and plums
It's fruity and juicy
And cool on your gums.
You say you've not tried it
I suggest that you do.
It's yummy for me
And you'll love it too.

Sophia McGonigle (9)
Ardstraw Primary School, Ardstraw

A Witch's Spell

A rat's guts spewing out
A troll's bogies
Tiger's eyeball
Lion's intestines
A monkey's head split open
A baboon with his leg chopped off
A mongoose who is split open
A hippopotamus' belly chopped up
A human's head split open.

Lewis Delphin (10)
Ashleigh Primary School, Barnstaple

The Race Of Time

Through the glistening snow I tread,
If I don't hurry the king will be dead.
Even though I'm very cold,
Still in my hand a note I hold.

In my view I see a castle's light,
In my hand I hold my note tight.
As the castle gates draw near,
My heart and soul fill with fear.

But what if I'm too late?
As I open the castle gate
I hear horses' hooves galloping towards me.
I turn around, there's a dark figure I can see.

I go in the castle as fast as I can,
But still behind me I can hear that man.
The man caught me,
The king is dead.
Now I'm in jail,
Hardly fed.

Rachel Jarvis (11)
Barker's Lane Community School, Wrexham

I Am . . .

I am red
Fire and lava.

I am sun
Scorching and hot.

I am a Big Mac
Tasty and tempting.

I am a dog
Fluffy and funny.

    I am . . .

Morgan Jones (10)
Barker's Lane Community School, Wrexham

I Am A Phantom
(Based on 'The Traveller' by Walter de la Mare)

I am old, from the 1600s to be exact
I float round day and night
I am lonely on my own
But there is a Traveller banging on my old house door
He sounds angry, angry as I am now
For someone sent me here hundreds of years ago.

I always feel anxious in my old house
In case another phantom will join me one day
Or will I be left alone for hundreds of years to come?

I am getting very annoyed now with the Traveller
As he is still banging and shouting at my old house door
I feel like opening the door right now
And shouting at him
But I cannot as I am a phantom.
Suddenly the Traveller pushes my old door open
And stares at my old, white face.

But it isn't a Traveller
I am staring at the Traveller's white face
And, *hurrah*, I am not on my own anymore
I have found my new fellow friend
I am sharing my old house with my phantom friend.

Stephanie Bellis (10)
Barker's Lane Community School, Wrexham

Chase

On my horse I go,
In the darkness of the night.
Bang! Bang! go the guns.
Once again they go.
The bangs startle my horse.
He runs faster and on we go.

I enjoy the excitement.
So does my horse
But I hope to finish the chase.
Bang! Bang! go the guns.
Once again they go.
The gems rattle in my pocket.
Scared they might fall out.

Home safe now with the prize.
Lost them miles away.
Bang! Bang! go the guns.
Once again they go.
Back on my horse I climb
And on goes the chase.

Rhian Davies (10)
Barker's Lane Community School, Wrexham

The Traveller
(Based on 'The Listeners' by Walter de la Mare)

There was a Traveller,
A Traveller wearing grey.
His green eyes sparkling in the moonlight.
He was carrying a message to an old friend.
He came to the house by the river on a horse,
A very big horse that was grazing in a field nearby.
He was knocking and knocking.
There was creaking on the veranda.
He waited and waited for someone to answer.
He knew someone was there
But they didn't answer.
The message was important.
A letter from the queen.
The Traveller was fed up.
He was thinking to come tomorrow
On his horse.
He knocked once more
And waited and waited
But no one answered
So he would return tomorrow.

Luke Davies (10)
Barker's Lane Community School, Wrexham

But Why?

He travelled half a mile.
But why?
He waited ten minutes.
But why?
He heard moans and groans.
But why?
No one answered the door.
But why?
The house was in the middle of nowhere.
But why?
There was no road whatsoever.
But why?
There was no noise at all.
But why?
He turns round and there is no horse.
But why?
He walks home on his own.
But why?

Are you puzzled? Yes!
But why?

Jason Daniels (10)
Barker's Lane Community School, Wrexham

The Traveller
(Based on 'The Listeners' by Walter de la Mare)

He comes on horseback with a clip-clop, clip-clop.
He knocks on the door but we do not answer
As we are scared of what he might do.

As the owls hoot in the darkness,
And the moon shines bright,
The Traveller stands and waits for a sound of us,
The Listeners.

We wait and listen for the Traveller to leave,
Finally he says his last words,
'Is there anyone in there?' and leaves.

The Traveller was a mysterious man
With a black hat, white cloak, grey eyes.
As the horse's hooves went clip-clop, clip-clop once again
We all knew he would be back with no doubt.

Sophie Davies (10)
Barker's Lane Community School, Wrexham

My Aunty Betty

This year my aunty Betty is taking me around the world,
To China, Mexico and maybe France.
Me and Aunty Betty are on our way,
We're heading for the north east today.

Since my aunty Betty was born,
She's always been up to see the dawn,
To see the world from night to night,
To see the mountains at their greatest height.

She climbed up the highest mountain,
There's so many things there's no point counting.
In India she ate a bug,
Back at home she ate a slug!

Ruth Cowlishaw (10)
Barker's Lane Community School, Wrexham

City Jungle
(Inspired by 'City Jungle' by Pie Corbett)

Snow splats down.
The motorway groans with all the heavy cars on his back.
The trees hug and shiver in the ice-cold rain.
Dustbins clang together with the shivering cold wind and rain.
Scrunched up newspapers with hands in their pockets
Trying to keep warm.
The phone box shivers and the phone says,
'Ha, ha, I'm nice and warm inside and you are ice-cold.'
Dogs and cats chase each other trying to keep warm.

Grace Wilkinson (9)
Beacon Primary School, Willenhall

Hell-Struck Dream

Heart thudding in my chest.
Little minions chaining me, pulling the chains,
Stopping my blood going round.
Saturated knives scratching through my skin inch by inch.
Sweat dripping from my head, slowly dripping.
I can feel fire burning my flesh, turning it to dust.
Smelling heavy smoke.
I was like a little chicken being cremated.
Wake, wake, I wish.
It's like a merry-go-round going round and round, never stopping.

Jack Williams (11)
Beacon Primary School, Willenhall

The Mud Of Clay Hill
(Inspired by 'Corky's Sewers' by Pie Corbett)

Some people say that it's really muddy
But I say it's a mud palace
Cos I am of a different persuasion

Some people say that it has really steep hills
But I say it's great for riding my bike down
Cos I am of a different persuasion

Some people say that you can trip over easily
But I say that it's great to ride your bike down the hill
Cos I am of a different persuasion

Some people say that it's got too many trees
But I say that it's a great jungle
Cos I am of a different persuasion
But no one cares.

Corey Reeves (10)
Beacon Primary School, Willenhall

The Dream Of Happiness
(Inspired by 'I Dreamed A Dream' from Les Misérables)

A warm breeze of happiness running down my throat
Like a drink of water,
Peace is flowing through me like a dream of love,
It's like an everlasting dream that will be mine only,
It's a dream about having a good life forever.

I feel like I'm wanted and belong in this world,
My heart beats as fast as a cheetah can run,
My dream of happiness is about having a good life forever
And being happy forever.
Dreams do come true.

Rebecca Murphy (10)
Beacon Primary School, Willenhall

A Fierce Dream

There he was tossing and turning from a fierce dream.
Devastation everywhere, guns blasting.
The tossing goes on.
Death filled the air.
Tanks roaring like lions.
The cold eating soldiers' flesh away
Bit by bit . . .

Adam Walton (11)
Beacon Primary School, Willenhall

City Jungle
(Inspired by 'City Jungle' by Pie Corbett)

The ants are swimming in the heavy rain struggling to get home
The sun beats down on the soft sand
The cars are saying, 'I hate snowy weather, it makes me miserable.'
The house is tired from standing in all sorts of weather
The black hole tunnel is like a giant elephant's mouth
And it's dark and goes on forever and ever.

Kieran Kendall (10)
Beacon Primary School, Willenhall

Dark Nightmare Dream

Robbers break in late at night
Right on twelve o'clock.
Creeping like mice in the black of night.
They scare me to death.
The rest of the tigers come down the dark, ghostly road
Fighting their way to the precious gold.

Adam Hampton (9)
Beacon Primary School, Willenhall

City Jungle
(Inspired by 'City Jungle' by Pie Corbett)

Trees shivering hard
The fences talking to one another
A car speeding with glee
Streetlights flashing when they are cold
The grass shrinking fast
Houses dancing like mad
Lizard cars crawling by
Scary dustbins clattering
Bridges breaking when they lay down
Books flying away
Cars smiling with yellow teeth
Cats speaking nastily
Robots singing loudly
The roads shaking wildly
The glass smashing off the rain
The cars running home
The sun bursting madly
Flowers dancing nicely
Dogs singing roughly
Pencils scribbling
Letters gliding across the floor
Fish swimming like people.

Terri-Leigh Sargeant (9)
Beacon Primary School, Willenhall

The Slave's Work

He sees the blocks bigger than him.
His eyes are swollen from sand.
Itchy and sore.
He moves the massive crane.

He feels the chains tear at the skin.
His feet are collapsing from joint overload.
He hears the rumbling of chains
As they begin to grumble.

Saul Rayner (10)
Beacon Primary School, Willenhall

Dream Of Being A Teacher
(Inspired by 'I Dreamed a Dream' from Les Misérables)

Pictures of being a teacher going round my head.
I tap my head to try to make it go away.
I hope one day I will become one.

I sit in the darkness looking out of the window
Wondering if I will become one.
I still see the pictures in my head
Still going round.
Cold going down my throat
Like ice cream slipping down.

I can see my future in my head.
My heart is beating fast.
I hope I will be one one day.
My spine shaking across my body
Like frost going down my back.

Nicole Painter (9)
Beacon Primary School, Willenhall

A Dream That Evil Came From Underground

Hell came back to kill us all
Lightning struck
None of us could tell what came back
Red tigers came and tore our world apart
We saw the tigers and I was stiff
I couldn't breathe
Red tigers came to my bedroom
And tore everything apart
The Earth was shrinking with every second.

Matthew Wilcox (9)
Beacon Primary School, Willenhall

Dream Of Peace

Peace lying with fear next to me,
Peace surrounded by love hearts covered in red,
Peace buried with anger and happiness with yellow flowers,
Peace coming alive next to me with love,
Peace staying still with ice melting.

Peace telling a dream to me with fire coming alive,
Peace coming towards me with knives,
Peace staying alive and still with happiness,
Peace creeping up to me with thunder,
Peace surrounding me like ghosts.

Ben Bates (10)
Beacon Primary School, Willenhall

My Dream Of My Life Job
(Inspired by 'I Dreamed a Dream' from Les Misérables)

It comes to me in the midst of night.
I dream the dream with such delight.
To be the greatest hairdresser.
Perms and spray fill the mind.
Silk and thick blonde and brown hair.
Chatter and cut and *snip, snip*.
Blower going, phones ringing.

Kayleigh Webster (9)
Beacon Primary School, Willenhall

City Jungle
(Inspired by 'City Jungle' by Pie Corbett)

Rain splatters off the ground.
Cars zoom past with a big smile.
Shivering trees wave to cars in a big pile.
Thin, tall lampposts stare as cars go past.
Dustbins stand in the cold rain waiting to be emptied.
Big, tall houses laugh and giggle as people walk past.

Abbie Myles (9)
Beacon Primary School, Willenhall

Jacqueline Wilson

I carefully turn the pages of my book,
As the rough texture rubs against my hands.

I take my biro and begin to write once more,
For twenty-three chapters left to write.

In the air I smell my book being published,
Now there are only a few chapters left.

I can taste the words as I mumble them out,
Then I quickly write them down.

I hear the sound of my pen in my mouth,
Clanking from tooth to tooth.

I see all of the joined up writing,
When I look back at my book.

It reminds me of my first book,
How relieved I was to get it published.

Natalie Stewart (10)
Beacon Primary School, Willenhall

Mrs Raybould's Den
(Inspired by 'Corky's Sewer' by Pie Corbett)

Some people say it is a messy place to be and it's muddy and slimy,
But I say it is nice and cosy,
Cos I'm of a different persuasion.

Some people say it rains a lot there and it smells and it is sludgy,
But I say it does not smell and it is not sludgy,
Cos I'm of a different persuasion.

Some people say there are spiders, slugs and snails,
But I say I don't care because I like slugs, spiders and snails,
Cos I'm of a different persuasion.

Ashley Maiden (9)
Beacon Primary School, Willenhall

Dreams
(Inspired by 'I Dreamed a Dream' from Les Misérables)

Appearing at night,
But not in the day,
Bright in the dark,
The moon is out.

Have some freedom,
Help people in need
Have clean air,
All children to have rights.

No more guns,
No more wars,
No bad words,
No more cruelty to animals.

Be healthy,
Treat others the way you want to be treated,
No domestic violence,
Be respectful to others.

Jessica Whitehouse (9)
Beacon Primary School, Willenhall

Dream Of The Peace

Peace filling every human with joy and laughter
Peace blowing to children to make happiness
Peace glowing at every mother and father brings a tear to their eyes
Peace staring them in the face trying to send a message
Peace getting the message through to the world
Peace making the little souls play to their hearts' content.

    Dream of the peace?

Rachel Grant (10)
Beacon Primary School, Willenhall

Dreams
(Inspired by 'I Dreamed a Dream' from Les Misérables)

Imagine, imagine hard,
See them at day,
See them at night,
Dreams are willing to come true.

As I silently fall to sleep,
I dream of peace,
No war,
Mystical creatures too.

Animals don't hurt,
Like they used to,
People care,
They love them so.

My dream fades,
I slowly wake,
I see the world's still the same,
Not like my dream.

Stevie Knowles (11)
Beacon Primary School, Willenhall

The Deadly FA Cup Final

I was playing in a game,
That's about the FA final,
I could blow a fuse any second now.
I could smell burgers, 'Mmmm,'
All I could taste was fresh air, 'Yuck,'
It reminded me of match days.
All I could see was the crowd in a blur,
I could hear the crowd cheering like animals,
The final score was 2-1,
We won.

Goal!

Adam Parsons (10)
Beacon Primary School, Willenhall

Dreams
(Inspired by 'I Dreamed a Dream' from Les Misérables)

Dreams come in the night,
Or during the day,
We dream of ambitions,
To come true.

Why the wars,
In the world,
With bullets and bombs?
Stop the wars and live happily.

Why the anger and hate,
To make people's lives a misery?
Stop the living disaster,
And don't make people upset.

I dream that,
Everyone will live happily,
And follow their ambitions,
To live a normal life.

Lauren Harris (11)
Beacon Primary School, Willenhall

My Dog Blue
(Inspired by 'Corky's Sewer' by Pie Corbett)

Some people say he's smelly and dangerous
But I think he's cute and cuddly
Cos I'm of a different persuasion.

Some people say he's a horrible creature
But I think he's as fluffy as pillows
Cos I'm of a different persuasion.

Some people say he's stupid and thick
But I think he's bushy and loony
Cos I'm of a different persuasion.

Jade Woolams (10)
Beacon Primary School, Willenhall

Dreams
(Inspired by 'I Dreamed a Dream' from Les Misérables)

They're all in your head,
They come when you're asleep,
They're always what you want to be,
So dream ahead and you will see.

You probably dream of world peace,
Or that you were a billionaire,
You'd rather be on a beach in Spain,
Not in England with the rain.

But then the nightmares start to come,
You think you're falling from a cliff,
Then you run but you don't move,
The glistening stars fall from the sky.

Your ambitions fall to pieces,
Your life's dream tears apart,
Life is now not worthwhile,
The nightmare breaks away your heart.

Aaron Chew (10)
Beacon Primary School, Willenhall

Fear In The Sky

Feeling fear following me in the dead of night
Feeling it killing me
The fear in the sky running away with it following me wherever I go
In day or night
Inside or outside
It did not care for wherever I go
See my friend
It follows me.

Arron Bates (10)
Beacon Primary School, Willenhall

Dreams
(Inspired by 'I Dreamed a Dream' from Les Misérables)

Appearing at night,
Or sometimes day,
Our ambitions,
Wanting to become true.

Peace,
No bombs,
Stop wars,
Stop domestic violence.

Love,
Kindness,
Friendliness,
Keep the loving feelings.

Fear,
Stop being scared of people,
No threatening,
Stop the hatred.

Having the time of my life,
Never giving up,
Being furtive,
Living in a world of candy.

Live to your heart's content,
Dance whenever you want, wherever you want,
No cruelty to animals,
All children must have rights.

Leigh Etheridge (10)
Beacon Primary School, Willenhall

Dreams
(Inspired by 'I Dreamed a Dream' from Les Misérables)

During the day,
During the night,
Our ambitions,
Bad and good,
Begging to come true.

Play games,
Stop wars,
No violence,
Cricket rules.

More chocolate,
More ice cream,
More sweets,
Less rats in the sewers,
Dreams are the best thing, don't lose them.

Alleigha Evans (10)
Beacon Primary School, Willenhall

Dreams
(Inspired by 'I Dreamed a Dream' from Les Misérables)

Appear at night,
As the sun comes round,
As your head hits the pillow there is no sound,
I dreamed a dream that is a fright.

They appear at night,
They appear in the day,
Whatever I do they don't go away.

They appear in the day,
As the sun comes up,
I dreamed a dream that didn't come true.

Lee Dougliss (11)
Beacon Primary School, Willenhall

World War II

Bombs, guns, swords and spears,
You could feel the black smoke,
Storm straight past your face,
Captain Stone crept around,
And you could hear the guns shooting,
And the swords clashing,
You could smell the Germans cooking their meal,
When you looked around,
You could see the Germans patrolling around,
Seeing the Germans eating the food,
You could taste the food and remind yourself
That you had food,
Ready in your barrack,
So you run back.

Joshua Bowker (10)
Beacon Primary School, Willenhall

My Dream
(Inspired by 'I Dreamed a Dream' from Les Misérables)

When the sky turns dark,
And I drift off to sleep,
My dreams start to appear,
I dream this one dream once every night.

All on one wish for it to happen,
I dream about no wars, no guns and no crying,
My dream has world peace,
But this country never will.

Some dreams won't come true,
And others won't fulfil,
Though simple ones have,
I guess this is as good as my world will get.

Lauren Deeming (10)
Beacon Primary School, Willenhall

Emotions

Sadness is blue like the tears of the ocean,
It feels like clear water running through your fingers,
It smells like the fresh, summer air.
It looks like a dull, drizzly day,
It tastes like bitter lemons,
It sounds like the ocean shells against your ear,
It reminds me of a dying soul.

Love is red like a blooming rose,
It feels like an affection for someone,
It smells like the scent of a sweet, sweet rose,
It looks like the beauty of a swan,
It tastes like the sweetness of ripe strawberries,
It sounds like a waterfall in a lover's world,
It reminds me of a marriage of happiness.

Bonnie Tsim (10)
Beacon Primary School, Willenhall

William Shakespeare

I am writing a play.
Feeling the tip of my quill, I write.
Smelling the ink from the paper, making me queasy,
Tasting the apple from my desk, eating while I write,
Reminds me of a kid writing his homework,
Thinking his brain out of his head.
Looking at the play at my desk called 'The Tempest',
Hearing the scribble of my pen as slow as I can.

Connor Lockley (11)
Beacon Primary School, Willenhall

Dreams
(Inspired by 'I Dreamed a Dream' from Les Misérables)

Appear at night,
Appear in the day,
It looks like a clear sight,
And then vanishes away.

No more wars,
No more stealing,
No more tours,
And no more dealing.

Want life to be happy,
With no bad words,
Want life not to be scrappy,
And no dead birds.

No more nits,
No more fighting,
No more hits,
And no more biting.

I hope all of these dreams come true.

Samuel Dewsbery (9)
Beacon Primary School, Willenhall

Love

Love is like red roses,
It smells like flowers,
It feels like Heaven,
It looks like friendship,
It reminds me of loads of small hearts,
It tastes like milk chocolate,
It sounds like the beating of a drum.

Emily Nicholls (10)
Beacon Primary School, Willenhall

My Dream
(Inspired by 'I Dreamed a Dream' from Les Misérables)

Appearing at night,
Appearing in the day,
It looks like a light,
Then it vanishes away.

Have freedom,
No bullying,
Do what you want,
And stop smoking,
Please.

No more wars,
No one to be poor,
No stealing,
Just change our
World, God.

Ellis Brookes (10)
Beacon Primary School, Willenhall

Gene Simmons

I ran on stage playing my guitar,
As I felt sweat running down my face,
I looked around me,
I could see the crowd jumping up and down
Like mad monkeys at the zoo.
I could taste my blood cups squirt fake blood from my mouth,
It smelt like sweaty feet,
It sounded like a big scream,
It reminded me of my first ever tour.

Zowie Rook (10)
Beacon Primary School, Willenhall

Dreams
(Inspired by 'I Dreamed a Dream' from Les Misérables)

In the night,
Appearing in light,
My target
Hoping to become true.

No conflicts,
Peace everywhere,
Stop fighting,
Delete all,
Please now.

My dream is, my dream is,
To be a . . .
Famous Warhammer painter,
And a cricket player,
I hope I could be these.

I hope all this will come true!

Nathaniel Holland-Bright (11)
Beacon Primary School, Willenhall

The City Jungle
(Inspired by 'City Jungle' by Pie Corbett)

Waste bins wandering around the streets eating glass bottles.
Snake cars sliding slowly down the dusty streets.
Shop doors opening like they are talking in the darkness of the night.
Fountains in the parks splashing around having such fun.
Trains running along the track like long centipedes.
Lorries striding down the street like a herd of elephants.
Newspapers rolling down the streets like pigs in mud.
Huge black towers looking around at things.
Streetlamps shining their bright eyes lighting the place up.

Callum Roberts (9)
Beacon Primary School, Willenhall

Dreams
(Inspired by 'I Dreamed a Dream' from Les Misérables)

Appearing in your head,
Blanking off your mind,
Your thoughts,
Trying to overtake your brain,
Waking people out of their sleep,
Only trying to make us wonder.

Wishing for peace and calmness,
Trying to be happy,
Thinking of no school,
Making homework blow.

Stopping people fighting,
No armies, so delighting,
No bullies,
That makes no violence flow.

We always dream of no bombers,
That we've got friends everywhere,
Peace over the world is an option,
That everyone wishes,
We want this all night,
Before we wake up.

If only I could win.

Liam Craig Allen (9)
Beacon Primary School, Willenhall

Dreams
(Inspired by 'I Dreamed a Dream' from Les Misérables)

During the day,
During the night,
Our ambitions,
Good and bad,
Wanting to come true.

No bombs dropping down,
No wars,
No fighting,
Peace.

No teachers,
No school,
No parents to shout,
Peace.

More candy,
More sweets,
More chocolate,
Peace.

Football games,
Cricket balls,
Netball tournaments,
Dreams,
Dreams.

Summer May Higgins (10)
Beacon Primary School, Willenhall

Ian Thorpe

I am diving into the pool,
I don't want to play the fool,
I'm in the relay,
There's no cause for delay.

I feel a bit frightened,
The lights have been brightened,
I can smell the rippling water,
I know my dad's up there with his daughter.

The water taste in my mouth,
In the water I'm heading south,
It reminds me of school,
As I slide into the pool.

When I look all around,
The most I can see is the ground,
I can hear the water wobbling,
I have got a stitch so when I get out I might be hobbling.

Nathan Mann (10)
Beacon Primary School, Willenhall

Dream
(Inspired by 'I Dreamed a Dream' from Les Misérables)

I wish I could be a world class fisherman,
Fish the Nationals
Win medals and trophies

But I know I am too young,
Even though I have won four championships
It's still not good enough because they're only
Junior championships.

I want to fish for England,
Fish mighty, great rivers,
And make my dad proud.

I will do this some day,
And then I will fulfil my dream.

Jordan Gary Hall (11)
Beacon Primary School, Willenhall

Dreams
(Inspired by 'I Dreamed a Dream' from Les Misérables)

Appearing at night,
During the day,
We dream dreams all through the day.

No more homework,
No more school,
No more violence in the world.

Loads more money,
Loads more sweets,
Loads more pets.

Better at netball,
Better at football,
Dad to come back and live with me,
Now all I dream is that my dreams come true.

Rheanne Griffiths (10)
Beacon Primary School, Willenhall

My Dreams
(Inspired by 'I Dreamed a Dream' from Les Misérables)

I dream in the day and in the night,
Dreams in the dark and in the light,
My dreams I wish to all come true,
Not just one but maybe two.

My dreams are good,
My dreams are bad,
My life is unfair,
It all turns bare,
Maybe I compare my life too fast,
To others' lives that will never last.

My dreams all turn to dust,
When I wake up in the morning it's far after dusk,
It's been such a long time so I can't remember,
It looks like there's going to be a change in the weather.

Charlotte Corbett (9)
Beacon Primary School, Willenhall

My Dreams
(Inspired by 'I Dreamed A Dream' from Les Misérables)

Don't smoke,
No wars,
Be one family,
No cruelty.

World peace,
All friends,
Be kind to one another,
No fighting either.

Treat others the way they treat you.

No weapons,
Clean air,
No violence,
Be happy.

No bad words,
Help poor people,
Keep healthy,
Dreams do come true.

Treat others the way they treat you.

Jamie Francis (10)
Beacon Primary School, Willenhall

Dreams
(Inspired by 'I Dreamed a Dream' from Les Misérables)

They may appear in the night,
And in the day,
But nobody will make them go,
Neither true.

Voices that just appear,
Voices that just go,
Nobody can change them,
As I say they are just dreams.

All we ask is for peace,
No fighting,
No wars,
Peace is all we ask.

Dreams are something,
That nobody can change,
Dreams,
Dreams,
Dreams.

Aaron Parry-Percox (10)
Beacon Primary School, Willenhall

Dreams
(Inspired by 'I Dreamed a Dream' from Les Misérables)

Coming in the day,
During the night,
Good and bad,
Coming true.

No wars,
Stop violence,
Help the homeless,
Peace.

Take away school,
Erase teachers,
Play games always,
Be silly.

Football games,
Cricket balls,
Netball tournaments,
Rounders bats.

Sabrina Wolverson (11)
Beacon Primary School, Willenhall

Our School
(Based on 'Our Street' by Les Baynton)

'Our school is not a quiet place,'
Say the chattering children, the clattering cutlery, banging trays.

'Our school is not a dull place,'
Say the painted walls, the colourful yard, the flower-filled garden.

'Our school is not a strict place,'
Say the wonderful teachers, the well behaved kids,
The caring parents.

'But our school is an exciting place,'
Says me!

Jessica Birch (8)
Bede Burn Primary School, Jarrow

I Wish I Could Paint . . .

I wish I could paint . . .
The fright on children's faces on Hallowe'en,
The delight of autumn's colourful leaves,
The sight of squirrels gathering nuts for hibernation.

I wish I could paint . . .
The howl of the wind rustling through the trees,
The brown owl hooting in the night,
The wildfowl flying around into the sky.

I wish I could paint . . .
The feel of a spiky horse chestnut shell,
The ideal, smooth conker,
The squeal of someone on Hallowe'en.

I wish I could paint.

Jennifer Parkins (10)
Bede Burn Primary School, Jarrow

I Wish I Could Paint . . .

The whisper of snow falling to the ground
I wish I could paint
The jingle of the bells ringing in the distance
I wish I could paint
The scent of the snow melting on your tongue
I wish I could paint
The flavour of Christmas pudding as it fills the air
I wish I could paint
The happiness of Christmas dinner.

Dale Brown (10)
Bede Burn Primary School, Jarrow

I Wish I Could Paint . . .

The ring of the church bell
The turn of the carol singers
The howl of the frost

I wish I could paint . . .
The twinkle in the stars
The gliding snow
The prickle in the holly bush

I wish I could paint . . .
The smell of roast turkey
The scent of dying flowers
The smell of burnt cake

I wish I could paint . . .
The snow melting on my tongue
Warm cocoa slipping down my throat
The yucky taste of sprouts

I wish I could paint . . .
The slide of the ice skates
The land of the snowflakes
The taste of hot chocolate.

Richard Dennis (10)
Bede Burn Primary School, Jarrow

Autumn Wonders

A rachnid web-swingers in wait on their webs,
U nderground the blind animals sleep like babies,
T he birds fly south for a warmer future,
U sing their brains the animals find food to survive,
M ist hangs like a ghost haunting a house,
N ow we shall all enjoy autumn as winter comes soon!

Nicholas Pallister (9)
Bede Burn Primary School, Jarrow

Winter

I wish I could paint
The smell of a Christmas turkey as it sizzles in the oven
The smell of a Christmas cake being cut for you to eat
The smell of a candle burning on Christmas Eve

I wish I could paint
The sight of a child playing in the snow-laden street
The sight of a bright light shining in the alleyway
The sight of a chilly snowman out in the cold

I wish I could paint
The taste of hot cocoa on a cold winter's night
The taste of tomato soup as I gulp it down
On an icy morning in winter
The taste of sizzling bacon in the pan on a cold winter's morn.

I wish I could paint but I can't.

Josie Miller (11)
Bede Burn Primary School, Jarrow

I Wish I Could Paint . . .

I wish I could paint
The sound of the robin whistling in the Christmas tree.
I wish I could paint
The taste of the soup going down me.
I wish I could paint
The smell of the frost hitting me.
I wish I could paint
The feel of snowballs hitting me.

Matthew Wood (10)
Bede Burn Primary School, Jarrow

I Wish I Could Paint . . .

I wish I could paint
The sight of a snowfall on a winter's day.
The flight of a snowball hitting you.
The fright of a snowman creeping up on you.

I wish I could paint
The smell of the Christmas dinner.
The smell of the figgie pudding.
The yell of 'Happy Christmas' throughout the house.

I wish I could paint
The taste of a figgie pudding.
The waste of alcohol from the night before.
The haste on my sister's face to open her presents at Christmas.

I wish I could paint
The grouch who got hit with a snowball.
The touch of snow from the sky.
The ouch of a hailstone hitting my face.

I wish I could paint
The sound of whirring breeze in my face.
The ground crunching beneath me.
The pound of my heart opening my presents.

Jack Davies (11)
Bede Burn Primary School, Jarrow

I Wish I Could Paint . . .

I wish I could paint
The scream of a child on a roller coaster ride
The giggle of a toddler going down the slide
The sizzling of burgers being fried

I wish I could paint
The sight of the log floats making a splash
The sound of the dodgems going smash
Let's get to the fair in a dash.

Kieran Day (10)
Bede Burn Primary School, Jarrow

Chilly Autumn Days

Leaves brown, yellow and gold,
Falling conkers big and bold.

Leaves crunching on the ground,
Big, thick scarves lost and found.

Wind whistling through big trees,
People with numb and shaky knees.

Horses shivering in their hay,
In chilly autumn days.

Ethan Nichol (9)
Bede Burn Primary School, Jarrow

A Day In Autumn

Lustrous, sparkling dew,
Continuous swirling fog,
Lips turning blue,
Leaves pile on the log.

Hedgehogs ready to hibernate,
Grotesque, glossy slug trails,
Spiders' webs on the gate,
Get wrapped up for winter gales.

Fred Davies (9)
Bede Burn Primary School, Jarrow

Winter Times

W ind rustling, will it blow?
 I cicle lakes shining with moonlight.
N earby stands a snowman, straight as a peg.
T rees misted with snow.
E vening ends, then gold and yellow sun dawns.
R obins singing in snowy trees.

Abbie Collis (9)
Bede Burn Primary School, Jarrow

Autumn Is Here!

Leaves crunching on the ground,
Conkers diving from the tree.
Fog walking not making a sound,
Autumn is here, come and see.

Frostbite is coming to town,
Animals hibernate all day long.
Get dressed warm, winter is coming,
Children playing and singing an autumn song.

Lewis Crooks (10)
Bede Burn Primary School, Jarrow

The Wind

Behold! The force I have, my unstoppable rage
Of gale and hurricane. The outstanding strength
And agility I possess, I use like fists of fury
Making a path of destruction wherever
I pass. Though sometimes I am calm
And gentle my force is like one
Million hands reaching out,
Stroking whoever lies
In my
Way.

Elliot Bridgewater (10)
Belle Vue Primary School, Stourbridge

I Am A Comet

Behold what speed I have.
Two opposite extremes of temperature,
Combined and harnessed onto a fist
Of ice and rock.
My hair, light-year long hair, streams behind me.
The beautiful colours of dye in my hair,
Light up the universe as I pass.
I speed towards the sun
And am then catapulted into the far reaches
Of the galaxy, on the second lap of the race.
On and on in the racing track I run.
In first place I am unbeatable.
And as I come close to the sun
My hair grows longer and more colourful.
My life is nearly over.
As I come closer my face starts to melt.
I will cross the finish, I will!
I slowly grow smaller, hot overpowers cold.
Closer and closer, I am still in first place.
Smaller I shrink, hotter I grow.
I am dead, my life is no more.
I have won.

Harry Thynne (10)
Belle Vue Primary School, Stourbridge

The Fire

Behold! The power I am!
Licking the logs with my boiling tongue,
Ever dreading my worst enemy, water.

I always reach out in an unstoppable rage,
Crisping the things that get in my way.
Black and grey are the ashes in my grate,
Dust and powder left to pile high.

The fingers of my flames slowly shrink back,
My hot reach begins to fade.
At my middle my heart glows orange,
Cooling the fire, now I am dying.

The last cracking sound I make,
Are my bones starting to break.
I'm just a heap of black and grey ash.
The wind carries my ghost high in the sky.

Hannah Potter (11)
Belle Vue Primary School, Stourbridge

Flames

Behold! The power I am!
I climb the walls and lick with my tongue
I dance and run as fast as I can
Through the woods on the time of the night
With the wind rushing through my unstoppable flames
As my arms are flying high with flames
Shooting off them like they were feathers.

So cool that I could fly high in the sky
With my arms flapping
With the like of a breath brushing across my face
With heat and warmth I feel cosy
With my legs just dangling, dangling high in the sky
And it was also swimming like a fish swimming,
Swimming deeply in the deep, blue sea.

Charly Wilder (10)
Belle Vue Primary School, Stourbridge

Fire

Behold! A ruler I am!
Destroying a house
Every sibling and spouse,
They see the power I have.

Like a robber I creep through each room
Licking the walls
Spitting on the floor
Leaving my mark as I go through.

My enemy alarms all life
I battle and run
For the games have begun
As they scream at the sight of my light.

Bethan Nutting (10)
Belle Vue Primary School, Stourbridge

The Sun

Behold! So large am I!
My fiery mass gives you puny people light,
My tongue licks out at the stars,
I'm so bright I'll blind you straight away,
Get the most out of me because I'll die in five million years.

Every thousand years or so,
Gleaming balls of rock and ice,
Come into my grasp and slowly disintegrate,
As they blast around my spectre,
I reach out with my fiery arms,
And digest them as I grow in size.

Luke Rowley (10)
Belle Vue Primary School, Stourbridge

Personification - Fire

Behold! The power I am!

I am leaping up this building like I have never leapt before.
I reach out with my fingers so that I can leap some more.

With my arms outstretched and my body poised
I now begin to make a noise.
I spit, I crackle, I give out a roar
Now my flames begin to soar.

The heat in here is so intense
The destruction caused makes no sense.
Who would have thought that a tiny flame
Would fast become a crying shame.

Charlotte Skelding (10)
Belle Vue Primary School, Stourbridge

Fire

Behold! The light I am!
I creep up the wall,
Like a cat burglar,
I spit and crackle,
Like a twig snapping,
I am used by humans to cook their food,
For I am the light of the world.

I hold back the darkness,
As I swim up the wall,
I reach out and grab,
Whatever I can,
For I am the heat of the world.

Sally Ovenall
Belle Vue Primary School, Stourbridge

Yuck

Yuck! Tomato soup!
Dinners are very smelly
Dinners are the best.

Chattering children,
Children running in the hall.
Shh! Now you've been told.

Daniel Phillips (9)
Bricknell Primary School, Kingston upon Hull

School - Haiku

Maths is so boring,
PE is so much better
Games is good as well.

Ryan Hirons (9)
Bricknell Primary School, Kingston upon Hull

Haiku

The playground is big
It's full of kids ev'ry day
It's a happy place.

Matthew McDougall (9)
Bricknell Primary School, Kingston upon Hull

Boring, Boring School! - Haiku

End of maths, hooray.
Science was very boring.
It's an awful day.

Jacob Green (10)
Bricknell Primary School, Kingston upon Hull

End Of School - Haiku

End of school, hooray
It has been a boring day
I can go home, yeah!

Sam Robinson (10)
Bricknell Primary School, Kingston upon Hull

Hymn Singing - Haiku

I love hymn singing,
Children singing happily,
In the hall we sing.

Isobelle Anderson (9)
Bricknell Primary School, Kingston upon Hull

The Playground Show - Haiku

Come on, let's go now
Time for the great playground show
Running, jumping, fun!

Calum Hart (9)
Bricknell Primary School, Kingston upon Hull

Mrs Weatley - Haiku

My teacher is kind
She teaches lots of children
She is so helpful.

Charlotte Hines (9)
Bricknell Primary School, Kingston upon Hull

Rugby Training - Haiku

Rugby training day
We get covered in the mud
Faces red and hot.

Louis West (9)
Bricknell Primary School, Kingston upon Hull

PE - Haiku

Bending and stretching
Now it is time for PE
Moving carefully.

India Robinson (9)
Bricknell Primary School, Kingston upon Hull

Haiku

Mr Brook is head
He is very busy now
He goes to classrooms.

Jason Young (9)
Bricknell Primary School, Kingston upon Hull

Lunchtime - Haiku

I love eating, yeah!
Lunchtime is my favourite,
I don't want to stop.

Charlotte Pickering (9)
Bricknell Primary School, Kingston upon Hull

The Playground - Haiku

The playground is loud
Children screaming and shouting
Children are lonely.

Lewis Turner (9)
Bricknell Primary School, Kingston upon Hull

The Playground - Haiku

I play with my friends
On the playground I do play
It is really fun.

Sophie Chapman (9)
Bricknell Primary School, Kingston upon Hull

Boring School - Haiku

School is so boring
I hope it's not on today
If so, 'Not going!'

Dan Jones (9)
Bricknell Primary School, Kingston upon Hull

Art - Haiku

It is art today
Splash of paint everywhere
Children going wild.

Amelia Wickenden (9)
Bricknell Primary School, Kingston upon Hull

School Days - Haiku

When we go to school,
We wear uniform to go,
We are proud and smart.

Natalie Bayley (9)
Bricknell Primary School, Kingston upon Hull

Assembly - Haiku

The proud, smart children
Sit on the wooden, hard floor
Singing a loud song.

Emily Walker (9)
Bricknell Primary School, Kingston upon Hull

The Playground - Haiku

The playground is big
Footballs bouncing heavily
Children racing fast.

Francesca Medcalf (10)
Bricknell Primary School, Kingston upon Hull

School

School is so boring
Especially wet playtimes
And so boring films.

Alex Donnelly (9)
Bricknell Primary School, Kingston upon Hull

Football In The Playground - Haiku

Someone pass the ball.
She shoots, she scores, it's a goal.
Kids playing football.

Rachel Innes (10)
Bricknell Primary School, Kingston upon Hull

Playground - Haiku

Little children fight
Teacher is laughing softly
Big kids playing ball.

Maya Singleton (9)
Bricknell Primary School, Kingston upon Hull

Packed Lunch - Haiku

Open the box now
What surprises are inside?
Crisps and sandwiches.

Dominic Slater (10)
Bricknell Primary School, Kingston upon Hull

Rugby - Haiku

Quick, fast and tackling
Rugby training is the best
Kicking and pushing.

James Wilson (9)
Bricknell Primary School, Kingston upon Hull

The Tiger

The tiger is proud
Of his work and
Muscular body. The tiger
Will pounce on its victim quicker than a flash.

He will run as
Fast as a carriage
And will send victims
To a sharp shriek.

The tiger is as
Big as an elephant
His teeth are swords
With a twitch of darkness.

He will belt you
Down and grate you
Into cheese. He will
Pounce quickly.

Theo Robson (10)
Brooke Primary School, Norwich

Charlie The Cat

As cuddly as a teddy bear.
As sweet as a piece of sugar.
As playful as a good toy.
As light as a small feather.
As small as a baby ant.
As cute as a little baby.
As soft as a comfy cushion.
As fluffy as a little fur ball.
As white as deep snow.
As playful as a football.

Joseph Bonner (10)
Brooke Primary School, Norwich

My Moggy

My cat is called Paws,
He scampers without a sound,
At night his eyes gleam,
As his silhouette barely marks the ground.
His fur looks like soot,
His paws are powder-white,
His miaow is a racket,
Especially at night.
He doesn't much like dogs,
And scratches their nose,
He despises being picked up,
And clings to you when you do.
His fur is silky,
And he purrs quite a lot,
He loves his cat biscuits,
And catches lots of mice.
His claws are pointed,
His teeth are sharp.
You may think he's an average cat,
But to me he's a *superb* pet to have.

Amy Gilks (10)
Brooke Primary School, Norwich

Hedwig

Barn owl,
Fluffy fur,
White as paper,
Swallows whole,
Eats mice,
Eats fast,
Flies peacefully,
Glides gracefully,
Lands softly.

George Saville (9)
Brooke Primary School, Norwich

Coco The Rabbit

His fur is sleek like velvet,
Dark and midnight black,
His tummy is white and fluffy,
All messy, scruffy and soft.

His eyes are protuberant and poppy,
Dark and chestnut brown,
His pupils are black and twinkly,
Like ebony stars in the sky.

He hops and bounces happily,
Like a black and shiny ball,
He springs, scrabbles and scrambles,
Hopping all over the grass.

His ears are velvet and pointy,
Pricked up like a pin,
Long, soft and sandy,
Listening for a rabbit sound.

He scampers without a sound,
At night his eyes gleam.

Helena Thomas (10)
Brooke Primary School, Norwich

Demon Cat

Proud as a peacock
He shows his fearsome glare
Eyes are as cold as the Devil's lair.

Creeping noiselessly,
His claws are as sharp as steel.
Crunching with his demon's teeth,
A mouse is his next meal.

Delicate fur like a baby's cheek,
Showing off his coat.
Quite like a venomous snake,
Showing slinky movements as he gloats.

Isobel Shaw Pritchard (9)
Brooke Primary School, Norwich

Stripes

At dawn in the jungle
A wild zebra came charging through
With a coat as smooth as silk and satin
And eyes as shiny as gleaming gems.

The zebra mane whipping in the wind
You can see the stripes flowing in the air
It's a walking, talking stripy carpet
The coat is like a black and white rainbow.

The zebra *stops*
It's as cute as a teddy bear
The zebra is as nice as yin yang
It's as stripy as a tiger.

The day goes on
The sun goes down
The zebra gets tired
So the zebra wanders back into the jungle.

Alice Martin (11)
Brooke Primary School, Norwich

Harry

The clumsiest cat that ever lived,
Owns a brain like a sieve.
Snores as loudly as my dad,
And eyes like murky sea.

He has pearly claws,
And a smooth, soft coat.
Tabby splatted fur,
Plus a nose that's salmon pink.

Paws like mini saucers,
And a lovely tiger's tail.
A very slow reactor,
Means a floppy, lazy cat!

Jessica Stanton (10)
Brooke Primary School, Norwich

Tigers

High jumping then on to foot to kill
Next secretly spying on animals
Ready to fight them catching food the only one
Chewing tasty food for life.

Feels so silky and so soft. Velvet
Covered coat
The stripes as black
As pitch-black night sky
And with sharp claws so dangerous
They could kill in just one touch
With orange blend in with black
And brings out the darkness.

Legs going fast like the wind
It moves so sly like a snake in the grass
Or walks so proudly without a care
In the world
Goes past the others just a pass.

Comforting home in the blazing sun
Kids are playing start to weep
Then rest for a little while
Last finally go to sleep.

Jenny Hill (9)
Brooke Primary School, Norwich

Hell's Cat

Bitten, sharp, pointy ears as white as clouds
Black and red eyes, from Hell's fireballs.

Black, sleek coat as black as coal
Stripes of black and white like a zebra's coat.

Long stripes of black with a dot of white
His feet are triumphantly plodding away.

This is the Hell's cat.

Katy Leeson (9)
Brooke Primary School, Norwich

The Springiest Dog Around

This creature springs joyfully on tiny feet,
Its dark, pleading eyes that sparkle like glitter,
Gaze into yours.

She gobbles food ferociously, with miniature jaws.
She's as small as a mouse,
As light as a feather.

Her smooth, silky coat,
Is as soft as velvet.
Her quiet bark that's just like a squeak,
Is going on all the time.

She's lively, bouncy, sparky, speedy,
And you can probably tell,
She's very energetic,
And the springiest dog around!

Julia Duncan (9)
Brooke Primary School, Norwich

Owls

Owls fly gracefully
Eyes as black as coal
Sleep peacefully
Eat as quiet as a rabbit
Deafening hoots
Hunt as quiet as a mouse

Fur as soft as velvet
Scared of noises
No one tells them what to do
Because they are king.

Alexander Jane (9)
Brooke Primary School, Norwich

A Journey To The Sea

On a golden, sandy beach
A little egg lay with a crack in the side.
Suddenly a little round head
As small as a ping-pong ball
Emerged from the creamy coloured egg.

Slowly it crawled out and started
To pull itself to the water's edge.

Its eyes were a grassy green
Its shell a chocolate brown
And dark green with a smear of
Fudge, rough and bobbly like a spot on
Your forehead.

As the pea-green flippers flipped the
Sand up into the cold, clear air the
Small baby turtle opened its tiny
Mouth and showed its microscopic
Teeth and let out a high-pitched
Screech.

The whole moon shone in the
Pitch-black sky as the baby turtle's
Head touched the ice-cold water for
The first time.

Slowly the turtle glided into the
Water.

With a silent splash he was gone.

Tortie Ward (10)
Brooke Primary School, Norwich

The Black Dog

The black dog's fur
Is as black as a
Chunk of coal
As she sleeps in
The dark night.

The black dog's heart is
As black as a dark night
And as cold as a piece of
Water ice.

As she stares down
At the icy cold ground
Below her, she pounces
Like a lion catching its
Prey.

Hollie Campbell (10)
Brooke Primary School, Norwich

Pepsi

Soft as a cat
Like a black, brown and white rainbow
Sleeps soundly.

Walks steadily
Trots briskly
Canters gracefully.

Jumps quickly
Snorts happily
Plods noisily.

Munches greedily
Relaxed as a rabbit
Cute as a cuddly bear.

Jessica Taylor (9)
Brooke Primary School, Norwich

Dolphins

Dolphins are graceful.
Dolphins are friendly.
Dolphins are clever.
Dolphins like to swim
Swiftly alongside boats.

Dolphins have small, beady eyes.
Dolphins have such velvety skin.
Dolphins have very long bodies.
Dolphins have the smoothest skin like a glass surface.

Dolphins love good company.
Dolphins have little, sharp teeth.
Dolphins are happy and free.
Dolphins hunt as fast as cheetahs.

Ellie Absalom (9)
Brooke Primary School, Norwich

The Gecko

At lunchtime my gecko goes out to eat,
She eats as quiet as a mouse.

Her back is as bumpy as a cat's eye
In the road

And her eyes are shiny and black,
Just like a gemstone.

Her tail is delicate like a vase
And her legs feel like bones.

My gecko's teeth are rocks,
Her tongue is as small as a spider.

She wriggles scarily and plods wildly.
Her tummy is as smooth as silk.

Matthew Boyle (9)
Brooke Primary School, Norwich

The Horse

She is a magnificent athlete.
Gallops as swiftly as the clouds,
She plods gracefully along with her head high,
Her mane flows like a flying flag.

She grazes happily whilst watching her horsy friends,
And munches as noisily as a small, round pig,
She sneaks treats from your pocket.

Her coat's as cosy as fluff but as shiny as the stars,
Her face is as pretty as a cluster of diamonds,
She is as brown as creamy, milk chocolate,
Her eyes twinkle as bright as the sun.

She stands as proudly as a lion,
As alert as a burglar alarm,
She stands as hopeful as a begging dog.

Rebecca Burrage (10)
Brooke Primary School, Norwich

The Fancy Mouse

He's a slave from the Underworld,
A warrior of stamina.
He's as furry as an ostrich,
He's as fast as an athlete,
He's as nippy as an ant,
He's as cute as a puppy,
He's as beautiful as a wild flower.
He's got fat, beady eyes,
He's got a big, shiny coat,
He's a cute cuddler,
A speedy runner,
A scuttly scuttler,
And he's my pet.

Daniel Earl (10)
Brooke Primary School, Norwich

Fat Cat

Our cat
Is fat
He can eat through a whole week's
Worth of meals in a day
He once stole a shocked neighbour's turkey
He's quite plump our cat

Our cat
Is contented
In the daytime he sits on the sofa
Going on the occasional plod about on his
Velvet paws
He's quite happy our cat

Our cat
Is sleepy
He sleeps all day, watching the world go by
Sleeping lazily
Eating and sleeping
He's quite lazy our cat.

Rosie Swain (10)
Brooke Primary School, Norwich

The Golden Monkey's Lunch

He swings from tree to tree
And then jumps heavily to the ground.
He screeches loudly at his mother
To let her know he's there.

He pesters his mother for his lunch
His hollow stomach starts rumbling
Like music bellowing in the distance
Until his mother throws him a green ball to calm him down.

He climbs then nearly slips
But climbs again to his leafy home.
His golden fur shines in the sun
While his teeth pierce through the ripe, green apple.

Jacob Clarry (10)
Brooke Primary School, Norwich

The Big Cat

He's a hurtling hunter,
He's a cowardless carnivore,
He climbs the tree elegantly,
He runs gracefully,
He's as cute as a gerbil,
But as vicious as a shark.
His fur is as sleek as a kitten's,
And as spotty as a Dalmatian's.
He lingers up trees,
He leers at his prey,
And pounces like a tiger.
His eyes are as shiny as the sun.
Have you guessed what he is?

A snow leopard!

Cameron Clarke (9)
Brooke Primary School, Norwich

My Polo

My pony is called Polo
He has a soft, dark brown coat
With a black mane and tail.
Polo is warm and cosy like a snugly bed.
He has four white socks like clean, fresh paper
And a splodge on his tummy like a tin of spilt white paint.
His eyes are shiny like green buttons.

He canters gracefully
Trots quickly
And walks slowly
He wouldn't hurt anyone.

Jessica Harmer (10)
Brooke Primary School, Norwich

Midnight Bibby

Bibby my cat has the eyes of an emerald,
They're big and they sparkle like glitter.
When she's scared her pupils blanket over,
They look like big, crystal black pearls.

Her tail swishes in the shape of a question mark,
In motion she moves elegantly,
Tiptoes out of sight,
She also waits for her master to admire her on her way off.

The fur on her skin, silky, smooth but short,
She has beautiful midnight-black fur
But her bib around her neck makes it look like the moon,
Although she's skinny she's cuddly too.

Bibby has a huge personality,
But her appearance is a mystery.

Mark Lawes (11)
Brooke Primary School, Norwich

The Hamster In His Cage

My hamster is cute
My hamster is small
My hamster is the skinniest of them all.

He's as soft as velvet
He's got mini teeth
He's smooth when you stroke him
And he likes to eat.

He's as soft as a cushion with elastic cheeks
He's black and grey
He's got weedy little feet.

He scurries like a rat
He does the monkey bars on his cage
He sprints on his wheel with a mini tail.

Ben Mitchell (9)
Brooke Primary School, Norwich

At The Bottom Of My Tray

At the bottom of my tray I found . . .

A slippery goldfish
And an old dusty bin.
A dead snake
And an old broken rake.
A smelly rat
And a lady's hat.
My pet dog
And a green frog.
Mary Poppins
And some birds' droppings.
A smelly, dirty ditch
And a big football pitch.

Alannah Sinnott
Brookside Junior School, Romford

At The Bottom Of My Tray

At the bottom of my tray I found . . .

A small grey mouse
And a cosy red house.

A bright coloured hat
And a black cat.

A shiny gold ring
And a proud king.

A red wrap
And a pink cap.

Abbie Tindall
Brookside Junior School, Romford

At The Bottom Of My Tray

At the bottom of my tray I found . . .

An old lady's hat
And a dead cat.
A big book
And a silver hook.
A shiny yellow moon
And a silver spoon.
An orange fish
And a dirty dish.
Green, slimy Flubber
And a dirty rubber.
A smelly sock
And a big clock.
A really big house
And a small grey mouse.

Danielle Downham
Brookside Junior School, Romford

At The Bottom Of My Tray

At the bottom of my tray I found . . .

A squeaky little mouse
And a tiny little house.

A pink baseball cap
And a red monster rap.

A pair of purple socks
And millions of cuckoo clocks.

A very rich king
And a really shiny ring.

A kicking football boot
And a train going *toot-toot*.

Courtney Jones
Brookside Junior School, Romford

Dreaming Of The Holidays

Going away from school
My brain is at its best
It's great, it's now a holiday
I think I need a rest

Sunshine gets in my eyes
I'll really need a hat
And this time for my brother
I'll take a cricket bat

I might go to Spain
Or France or Italy
Or maybe further oast
To Northern Germany

How might I travel
By boat, car or train
Or maybe I'd go by air
Perhaps by aeroplane

I wonder what I'll do there
At the hotel or on the beach
Be active or relax
Or swim way out of reach

I'd really want to stay there
I'll really hate to go
I'd fly back to Scotland
But I really can't say no.

Thomas Bartos (9)
Buckstone Primary School, Edinburgh

Hurricane

Hurricane, you have a violent wind,
We don't want you to stay,
Your destruction causes flooding,
Drowning and deaths.
You cause damage and hatred,
You are intense and you harm,
You cause havoc in parts of lands,
Everyone is concerned about their family,
Please go away soon, our land has been disturbed,
I hope you will not stay any longer!
I shall hide in a corner, hoping I will be able to see my family -
Soon.

Amy Galbraith (9)
Buick Memorial Primary School, Cullybackey

The Terrible Tornado

Hide, hide, the tornado is coming,
Hide, hide, you'd better start running!

Run away, run away, it's going to hit the state,
Run away, run away, before it's too late!

Whirling and twirling, it's spinning here fast,
Whirling and twirling, let's hope it goes past!

The tornado is here!
The tornado will spread fear!

Finally, the tornado has spun by,
Finally, I'm glad no one had to die!

Adam Greer (9)
Buick Memorial Primary School, Cullybackey

Snowing

Snowing, snowing
1, 2, 3
It's going to be fun,
Wrap up warm . . .
Or you will get cold,
Beware! Jack Frost, the feet nipper!
The things I'm going to need are -
One snowman to guard my igloo,
An igloo for under cover,
Snowballs in case my enemy tries to attack me.
Hopefully my snowman will watch out for them!

Natalie Swann (9)
Buick Memorial Primary School, Cullybackey

Snow

Snow, snow, what about snow?
It can make the children laugh and cry.
It falls from the sky.
The drivers hate it.
The children playing in the wonderful snow.

Snow, snow, what about snow?
It is dangerous as well as fun.
It can cause people to crash
As well as having fun.
It is sad having to see it go.

Bethany Coulter (9)
Buick Memorial Primary School, Cullybackey

Tsunami

It all starts with a little crack,
Then a crumble, then a shatter, then a bang!
The violent earthquake has begun,
With a slash and a crash,
The horrendous wave has started.
It's at a very great height,
It's coming to the land.
The cries and shouts of sadness.
The wave has hit land,
There are dying, drowning people,
Leaving our world.
The murder of this wave is done.
They are dead.
That is the tsunami.

Charles Orr (9)
Buick Memorial Primary School, Cullybackey

Snow

The snow was coming in grey and white
It was falling all through the night
It was such a sight when it covered
The fields in white
It sealed up the pond for a week and a day
But it was such fun playing in snow.

Matthew Beattie (10)
Buick Memorial Primary School, Cullybackey

The Sun

In India it is hot,
Here it is not.
All the water is gone,
They are all thirsty,
So am I.
I have a bottle of water,
It is very cold,
I am going to drink it all.
Or will I have to share it?
The good things about the sun are
The beach,
The swimming pool,
Dogs barking . . .
I like the sun.

Luke Henry (9)
Buick Memorial Primary School, Cullybackey

Snow

Winter is near, come and cheer.
See the snowflakes falling so sweetly,
Hear the children laugh and play,
See the frozen drops sparkling in the distance.
Children running round the house,
Looking for winter hats and scarves.
All the children out at night having a snowball fight.
Mums are reading little books to their children.
For now, all the snow and Christmas cheer
Has gone away for another year.

Gemma McClenaghan (9)
Buick Memorial Primary School, Cullybackey

The Hurricane

The hurricane swept this way and that,
Lifting up buildings, destroying the land.
A cool breeze turns to an overwhelming blast, just like that.
People praying for their lives.
Even the strongest buildings stumble at the hurricane.
We couldn't hear each other cry
Over the furious winds.

You can finally hear the tragic screams,
Death was calling.
In the distance babies cry, without answer.
The hurricane has done its deed,
The houses collapsed and people trapped.
The ones who survived maybe, just maybe,
Wish they hadn't.

Michael McKelvey (10)
Buick Memorial Primary School, Cullybackey

The Storm

It was a very funny day,
It started very sunny.
We were coming from the park,
Going to the car.
The flash of anger.
It was like Germany turned into the land of evil.
It was like a frown of God.
It was like a monster in the river.
Three drowned, but the rest survived -
A true story.

Daniel Bestek (9)
Buick Memorial Primary School, Cullybackey

Inside A Dancer's Head

I see the stage that I'm about to go on
Rows of audience waiting there
Shining, black tap-shoes on my feet
A judge sitting stiffly on her chair.

People in the audience talking
The clang of the ringing bell
Jazz music from the CD playing
The clack of my shoes tapping well.

My dress tickling my legs
Butterflies making my tummy quake
My feet moving so quickly
But nerves making my legs shake.

Chloe McAleese (9)
Buick Memorial Primary School, Cullybackey

Cocker Spaniel

Children are skipping and playing about
The cat is playing with my ball
My toys are lying in my bed
Other dogs are barking behind the wall.

Now the cat is purring
Music is playing while children dance
The other dogs are snoring while they sleep
Nobody even gives me a glance.

The rain is dripping on my head
A butterfly is sitting on my nose
I am hungry and it is teatime
Will they remember, do you suppose?

Ellen Dunlop (8)
Buick Memorial Primary School, Cullybackey

A Child On Christmas Eve

Stockings on the end of the bed
Christmas lights that sparkle
Decorations all around
And gifts for you and me
Under the huge tree.

Dad and Mum talking
The fire going out
Me getting a carrot out of the fridge
Thinking of Jesus' birth
Bringing peace to all the Earth.

Excited, for tomorrow is Christmas
Worried that I have not been good
Anxious to get what I asked for
Scared in case I don't get to sleep
But wanting a little peep!

Nicola Anderson (8)
Buick Memorial Primary School, Cullybackey

The Tabby Cat

Scratching on my scratching post
Playing with my wool
Listening to my owner
Running round the stool.

Scared when the dog barks
Sleepy every night
Happy that my food is Whiskas
And they stroke me right.

A saucer of milk
The warm, cosy fire
A soft-made bed
What more could I desire?

Janessa Morgan (8)
Buick Memorial Primary School, Cullybackey

A Jack Russell

I play with pegs in the garden
There's that cat! *Bark! Bark! Bark!*
Running with my mistress
I can see goldfish in the pond in the park.

I hear my master snoozing
And birds cheeping while I creep
I step on leaves - *crunch, crunch* they go
A greedy eye on my bowl I keep!

It's lovely when I get patted
I like to feel the wind on my fur
The heat of the sun makes me tired
I feel a sleep coming on - *grrr.*

Georgina Shaw (8)
Buick Memorial Primary School, Cullybackey

England Versus Northern Ireland

Black and white ball
Paul Robinson in goal
England players get the ball
In the back of their net.

Referee blows his whistle
Boos of the people from England
Cheers from the Northern Irish crowd
Players run to the centre so proud.

All the players tackling hard
Time's going on - can we really win?
Such excitement, such a thrill
Northern Ireland win one-nil.

Luke Simpson (9)
Buick Memorial Primary School, Cullybackey

Conversation With A Tree

Child: What can you see?

Tree: The birds circling in the sky
Colourful leaves on my branches high
Children playing games all around
Dry autumn leaves piled on the ground.

Child: What can you hear?

Tree: The singing birds on my branches, see
The passing wind flowing gently by me
Rabbits below - I hear scampering feet
And busy traffic travelling on the street.

Child: What can you feel?

Tree: Water travelling to my leaves from my roots
Birds perching amongst my twigs and fruit
My branches bending against the wind from the west
And a squirrel climbing up my trunk to its nest.

Timothy Spence (9)
Buick Memorial Primary School, Cullybackey

Tony Hawk (A Famous Skateboarder)

Tony, I like your stunts
Nose-grind and somersaults
If you fall you don't care
Soon you'll be back in the air.
You feel the board at your feet
As you jump the kerbs along the street
You can jump off a high wall
But there's nothing worse than a bad fall!

Craig Coates (9)
Buick Memorial Primary School, Cullybackey

Henrietta's Hockey Hit

Henrietta hits a whopper, whizzing ball
With her super-duper hockey stick
Her family is watching from the side
She dribbles round the opposition quick

There is a noisy slap of hockey stick
Against the teeny-weeny ball
The crowds are screaming in Henrietta's ear
The coach shouts loudest of them all.

Henrietta feels cold with her skirt on
And her T-shirt is so light
But she feels competitive and a bit worried
She feels that she should, could, might . . .

She takes careful aim
She wins the game!

Rhianna Campbell (8)
Buick Memorial Primary School, Cullybackey

Swimming Lessons

I see . . .
The water bobbing up and down
The splashes going over my head
My goggles steaming up
Bubbles moving around the pool

I feel . . .
The nose plug tight across my nose
The goggles stuck on my eyes
The warm water against my back
The vibrations in the water

I hear . . .
My teacher shouting at us
The splashing of other people's feet
My breath, heavy breathing
The buzzer to signal time is up.

Robbie Campbell (9)
Buick Memorial Primary School, Cullybackey

Thoughts From The Pitch

I see . . .
Opponents better than I could be
A stadium much bigger than me
The sphere-shaped football
The referee - boss over all!

I hear . . .
People shouting us on and cheers
Rain pouring on my head and ears
Commentators telling the crowd through mikes
Whistles blowing for free kicks.

I feel . . .
Nervous in case they score
Great because we've scored once more!
Cold because it's raining and wet
Tired and gasping for every breath I get.

I smell . . .
Smoke from cigarettes
Chips that the crowd gets
Hamburgers covered with red ketchup
Victory - it's the last minute - we're two up!

I hope
We win because we deserve to
And because our manager wants us to
The fans will leave, glad to see
The winning goal scored by me!

Ben Gaston (8)
Buick Memorial Primary School, Cullybackey

The Nightmare

My mum tucks me up in bed
Bright stars twinkle above my head
Outside, the dark and misty sky
Beautiful flashes of fireworks high.

Owls hoot from a tree branch bare
Foxes howl on the moor out there
Fireworks sparkle and bang away
I hear footsteps coming my way.

Under the door, light makes a line
Quivers go creeping up my spine
I imagine a ghost poking my shoulder
Under the quilt my hands feel colder.

What will happen now, I fear
Will the ghost get me if it's near?
If the lights go off, I won't see
Will anyone come here with me?

What's that noise? I feel a shake
I hear a voice, I start to quake
'Wake up, darling, you're quite alright
You're having a dream, it's the middle of the night!'

My mum and dad are smiling down
And my little sister, Katy, in her dressing gown
They give me a great big hug and they care
To make me forget *a horrible nightmare.*

Alana Duff (8)
Buick Memorial Primary School, Cullybackey

The Tree Of Life

God made the wonderful trees
They have some pretty colourful leaves
I know the family plum tree
Which gives plums so sweet for tea.
There is a little apple tree
Just across the road from me
I look at the high leaves
As I see them swaying in the breeze.
In autumn leaves are orange, red, yellow and brown
On a breezy day they come fluttering down.
There is a most wonderful tree
If you climb up it, the village you can see.
I have a friend - she is a tree!
In her branches we can play, you and me.

Nicole Paul (9)
Buick Memorial Primary School, Cullybackey

Harry Potter's Owl

Ron cleaning his robe
Letters being tied to other owls in the hall
Harry sitting at his desk writing
Quidditch robes hanging from the wall.

Professor McGonagall telling Malfoy off
Harry, Ron and Hermione quietly speaking
The wind whistling through my window
As the boys go to bed, old mattresses squeaking.

Warmth as I enter the room after my message
Harry's trust I understand
Tired after the long journey
Glad of the gentle pat from his hand.

Bryony McCleery (9)
Buick Memorial Primary School, Cullybackey

My Funny Family

My mum is such fun
You don't know what she's like
We go shopping together
We're like best friends.

My dad is so funny
He said I'm his honey
He's so good at football and supports Leeds.

My little sister is a twister
You don't know what she's like
But we get along
She's the best friend you could get.

My big brother, you don't know what he's like
Because he changes every minute
But all I know is that he supports Man Utd.

Altogether, we have such fun
In one big happy family.

Lauren Perry (9)
Buick Memorial Primary School, Cullybackey

Grim Reaper

Bloodshed all around
People screaming as I kill more
Hate rushing through my veins
The black hood hiding my face
My hand touching the cold axe
Bones dropping or hitting walls
The axe wiping out all mankind
The fiery ghost of doom
Darkness through day and night
The urge is trying to tell me
I should kill more!

Stuart Wylie (8)
Buick Memorial Primary School, Cullybackey

Best Friends

Jodie is very funny,
Jodie likes football,
She is my friend.

        Carly is a good friend,
        She plays with everybody,
        She likes football.

Megan likes football and hockey,
She has long hair,
Megan has brown eyes.

        Lynsey has brown hair,
        She likes cats and dogs,
        She has a cat.

Ruth lives on a farm,
She has a brother and sister,
She has a go-kart.

        Me, I live on a farm,
        I play hockey and football,
        I have two sisters,
        I like my quad.

Jessica Reid (10)
Buick Memorial Primary School, Cullybackey

My Trees

I love trees
I like their leaves
They give us food
Which is very good
Don't cut them down
Or I will frown.

Jordan Campbell (9)
Buick Memorial Primary School, Cullybackey

My Pet Rabbit

I like feeding my rabbit, it's such fun.
Every day when I come home, I pet her.
I love my rabbit to pieces.
I would never let anything happen to her.
I call her Charlie, she will soon be having babies.
I used to play with her in the house,
But now she lives in a hutch in the back yard.
All she does is eat and sleep,
But I still love her.
Even if she has babies, she will be my special rabbit.
She hates other people going near her.
She likes me petting her under the chin.
When I first got her, she sniffed me.

Kurtis Given (9)
Buick Memorial Primary School, Cullybackey

My Dogs

My dogs are cute and playful,
They pant and woof all the time.
I have two dogs, one called Ben,
Who always lies in the middle of the floor.
The other is Gabby, she's so small people stand on her,
She stays in bed all day.
Me and my mum take them for a walk every day.
I feed them all the time.
Me and my mum bath them too.
Gabby's age is 14, Ben is five years old,
But they're always on the go.

Charlotte Carney (9)
Buick Memorial Primary School, Cullybackey

Crazy Dog

I have a Doberman, she is one and a half
Her name is Tess, she is a laugh.

She is big and crazy
And loves to eat daisies.

She's fast, she's strong
She's scary, but we get along.

Tess is playful
And as crazy as a bull.

She eats and bites
She jumps and fights.

I have a crazy dog
Oh no!

Megan Rea (10)
Buick Memorial Primary School, Cullybackey

Friendly Pets

Dogs go *woof, woof* a lot
You can pet them
A dog pants when it is out of breath
Dogs are friendly sometimes

Fish swim about
They eat fish food
They hide behind algae

Lizards stay still
Skin sheds
Lizards eat crickets
Lizards have scaly skin.

Reuben Lamont (10)
Buick Memorial Primary School, Cullybackey

Super Hero

Oh, how long I've dreamed of being a super hero,
Tornado Boy with magic whirls and whirl guns,
Twisting round like a hurricane,
But staying on the ground like a tornado.
For I am Tornado Boy,
With my side-kicks Hurricane Girl and Wind Woman,
Flying through the air,
Meeting Batman, Robin Hood and the Crimson Chin.
For I am Tornado Boy!
Capturing villains like Venom, Dr Doom
And the Evil Tabacia, my fierce enemies.
Saving Leroy the Mayor, Jordan the Butler,
Using amazing powers!
But dreams are for men,
For I am Tornado Boy no longer.

Matthew McCallion (9)
Buick Memorial Primary School, Cullybackey

Pets

Dogs bark and they growl,
They pant after a long walk
They wag their tails when they're happy
And lick you.

Parrots fly
From one place to another
They eat crackers
And grapes as well.

Cats climb up trees
They chase birds
They wag their tails when they are mad
They purr when they're happy.

Robbie Moore (9)
Buick Memorial Primary School, Cullybackey

Tornadoes

Whirly, burly, curly, twirly
Tornadoes!
Strong, long, fast, tall
Tornadoes!
Jumping, clasping, sucking, waving
Tornadoes!
Small, short, high, low
Tornadoes!
Smashing, bashing, thrashing, clashing
Tornadoes!

Thomas Mellon (9)
Buick Memorial Primary School, Cullybackey

What Is Weather?

What are clouds for?
They're for the gods to sit on.

What is thunder?
The gods having a tantrum.

What is lightning?
The gods having an argument when sparks are flying.

What is sleet?
The gods sneezing.

What is rain?
The gods crying.

What is snow?
The gods' dandruff.

What is fog?
The steam from the gods' shower.

Elyse Miller (11)
Burray School, Orkney

Weather

What is snow?
Snow is white,
Soft as rabbit's fur.

What is thunder?
Thunder is frightening,
It's loud as a house falling down.

What is lightning?
Lightning is bright,
It's a torch flashing off and on.

What is rain?
Rain is droplets,
It is as big as peas.

What is wind?
Wind you can't see,
It is as strong as a bulldozer.

What's your favourite weather?

Cheryl Smith (11)
Burray School, Orkney

Disastrous Weather!

What is thunder?
It is pigs crashing on some drums.
What are twisting tornados?
They are water going down the plughole.
What are clouds?
They are fluffy white sponges.
What is a blizzard?
It is little bits of fluffy snow.

Stefan Taylor (11)
Burray School, Orkney

Weather Poem

What is a blizzard?
Hard snow smashing everywhere.

What is rain?
Driplets of drops falling from the moonlit sky.

What is sunshine?
The clouds going away and a round, hot, shiny sun breaking out.

What is snow?
Flakes falling down soft and gentle on your shoulder and making
you shiver.

What is ice?
It's cold and chilly and you slip and slide and your bottom gets wet.

What is hail?
Strong pellets on you, with stabs poking you in the back.

What is sleet?
It is a slushy drink that turns to water.

Claire Corsie (11)
Burray School, Orkney

Shadow

Shadow shimmers into our reality like rippling water
He looks to see the dimming light with violet eyes
During day he seeks refuge in the shadow realm, the opposite
of ours
But now it is his kingdom of time, ruling all darkness.

Shadow is strengthened by the darkness as am I
His thin, pale face glaring always
His fingers wrapped around the last speck of light, diminishing it
Plotting in a limitless mind, devising new ways of banishing light.

Ethan Prior-Sanderson (11)
Burray School, Orkney

What Is Night?

Night is a Miss Stanger
She makes me really good inside
And very happy, like a cuddle from my mum.

Her face looks smiley, like my teddy bear
Her eyes are like two baby kittens
Her hair is like the big, shiny moon
Her clothes are made of cotton
Like a wild rabbit's tail
When she moves
She is a beautiful owl
When she speaks
Her voice is like a smooth horse's mane
She lives in a palace with her sister
And the shimmer of the moon follows her around.

Night comforts me.
Grace Corsie (9)
Burray School, Orkney

Night

Night is like a fairy of lightness
She makes me feel so cheerful
Her face looks like a white, sparkling moon
Her eyes are bright, like sparkling stars
Her mouth is a half-moon smile
Her clothes are made of white owls' feathers
When she moves, it's just like a swooping bird
When she speaks, it's just like a twinkling star
She lives in a sparkling castle with fairies and flying pigs
Night likes me.

Erin Smith (9)
Burray School, Orkney

Weather

What is lightning?
A dodgy line in the sky.
Where does it start?
Does it petrify you?
It petrifies me.

What is thunder?
It is a sound in the sky.
I shiver in my bed.
It sounds like something roaring.
I feel like going under my cover.

What are snowflakes?
They are a pretty shape.
They are ice-cold.

What is wind?
It is a breeze.
It is like a giant blowing.

David Sinclair (9)
Burray School, Orkney

Dragon Slumber

Dragon curled up warm
Warm but pointless lies treasure
Beneath the dragon
Fire glows bright in the darkness
Dragon wakes from its slumber!

Ruairidh Gough (9)
Burray School, Orkney

I Shall Not Sleep

The night is still
And shallow depth,
The darkness fails with a moonlit sky.

The owls hoot,
The cobwebs glow,
The icy mountains covered in snow.

The sky is kind
The night is bold
Such comfort in the moonlit sky.

The sky is safe
The guardian's watching, listening
When morning comes, night's hidden in the mountains.

The night is still
And shallow depth
The darkness fails with a moonlit sky.

Connor Malloy (11)
Burray School, Orkney

Threatening Thunder And Lousy Lightning

What does thunder and lightning sound like?
It sounds like the waves crashing and smashing on the beach.
What does lightning look like?
A shiny gold fork on a dark, dark night,
With a glaze of moonlight sparkling on it.
How long does it last?
I don't know.

Shannon Hume (11)
Burray School, Orkney

Night Poem

The owl of night,
He vanishes by day,
He brings the darkness
To find his prey.

A soft, silent figure,
Moves through the sky,
No one has seen the owl
But I.

The misty, muffled
Cry in the night,
He has found his shadow
And hides there from fright.

Then he comes out
And flies again
He swoops and swerves
And cries now and then.

The owl of night,
He vanishes by day,
He brings the darkness,
To find his prey.

Lily Humphreys (10)
Burray School, Orkney

What Is A Snowflake?

A snowflake is a dove
Shining in the sky.

A snowflake is a light
Shining tinsel round your neck.

A snowflake is a silky diamond
Hitting the ground.

A snowflake is a splat of paint
Hitting the white earth.

Matthew Broadhurst (9)
Canon Maggs CE Junior School, Bedworth

What Is A Snowflake?

A snowflake is a falling star
Gliding across the sky.

A snowflake is a hovering dragonfly
Swooping across the river.

A snowflake is a long, silver piece of tinsel
Hanging from the top of the Christmas tree.

A snowflake is a sparkling, white diamond
That falls from the heavens and settles gently on the ground.

A snowflake is an angel sent from God.
It floats to the ground and shimmers in the light.

Georgia Snaith (9)
Canon Maggs CE Junior School, Bedworth

What Is A Raindrop?

A raindrop is a shiny, blue fish,
Galloping through the sparkling water.

A raindrop is a blue flower lying in the sun,
Swaying in the breeze.

A raindrop is a sparkling diamond,
Shining in the orange sun.

A raindrop is a bright, yellow star,
Lighting up in dark space.

A raindrop is a see-through, multicoloured bubble,
Floating through the air.

Christopher Snaith (9)
Canon Maggs CE Junior School, Bedworth

What Is A Snowflake?

A snowflake is a white dove
Gliding gracefully on blue water

A snowflake is silver tinsel
Shimmering in the darkness

A snowflake is a piece of ice
Falling down, down, down

A snowflake is a small star
Glowing all night long

A snowflake is a crystal
Rolling on the floor.

Bethany Draper (9)
Canon Maggs CE Junior School, Bedworth

What Is A Snowflake?

A snowflake is an angel, pure as a jewel,
Floating onto silver ground.

A snowflake is a diamond dragonfly,
Flying through the air.

A snowflake is a milk top,
Melting away.

A snowflake is a pure white dove,
Gliding gracefully through cold air.

A snowflake is a silver light,
Lighting up the world.

Shannon Reade (9)
Canon Maggs CE Junior School, Bedworth

What Is A Snowflake?

A snowflake is a pure, white dove
Drifting through the silky sky.

A snowflake is a crystal jewel
Dropping down to Earth.

A snowflake is silver lace
Gliding up to Heaven.

A snowflake is a lightly frozen leaf
Fluttering across the frozen sea.

A snowflake is dark, white paint
Dropping off the dark, green tree.

Paige Johnson (9)
Canon Maggs CE Junior School, Bedworth

What Is A Snowflake?

A snowflake is a pure, white dove
Flowing above the water.

A snowflake is a broken bit of ice
Dropping down to Earth.

A snowflake is a frozen leaf
Drifting through the sky.

A snowflake is a crystal
Gliding through the air.

A snowflake is a butterfly
Fluttering from a blueberry.

Amy Brown (9)
Canon Maggs CE Junior School, Bedworth

What Is A Snowflake?

A snowflake is a small petal
Swerving to the frosty ground.

A snowflake is a silver star
Shooting through the night sky.

A snowflake is a great big smile
Spreading to all around.

A snowflake is a diamond
Falling from the sky.

A snowflake is a lily
Spreading to every field.

Katie Molesworth (9)
Canon Maggs CE Junior School, Bedworth

What Is A Snowflake?

A snowflake is a glamorous white swan
Flying the clear, blue sky.

A snowflake is like an angel
Falling from the sky.

A snowflake is like frost
Covering the grass.

A snowflake is like a polar bear
Resting its eyes.

A snowflake is a wonderful diamond
Lying in a shop.

Jacob Morson (9)
Canon Maggs CE Junior School, Bedworth

What Is A Snowflake?

A snowflake is a shimmering star
Twinkling brightly over blue water.

A snowflake is bright, silver tinsel
Falling from high in the silver-blue sky.

A snowflake is a golden pawprint
Marked in a blue puddle.

A snowflake is a silver bead
Falling into a silver-blue puddle.

A snowflake is frozen leaves
Falling from a tree.

Pagan Conroy (9)
Canon Maggs CE Junior School, Bedworth

What Is A Cloud?

A cloud is a fluffy piece of candyfloss
Dropping into a small puddle.

A cloud is a clean, white sheep
Bouncing up and down.

A cloud is a lovely feather
Floating down and down.

A cloud is a springy marshmallow
Falling on a blue carpet.

A cloud is a cuddly cushion
Lying comfortably on the settee.

Joshua Bagnall (9)
Canon Maggs CE Junior School, Bedworth

What Is A Snowflake?

A snowflake is a shining, silver bead
Floating down from the clouds.

A snowflake is a twinkling, golden star
Shooting from the black galaxy.

A snowflake is a magic butterfly
Fluttering down from the gardens of Heaven.

A snowflake is a golden crocodile's tooth
Falling down from the blue beyond.

A snowflake is a bright, shining light
From the halos of the good angels.

Daniel Day (10)
Canon Maggs CE Junior School, Bedworth

What Is A Snowflake?

A snowflake is like a peaceful shard of ice
Fluttering down gracefully to the snow angel.

A snowflake is like a gem
Shining like light.

A snowflake is like a dove
Covered in a silky veil.

A snowflake is like a dash of paint
Falling from Heaven.

Lewis Herdman (10)
Canon Maggs CE Junior School, Bedworth

What Is A Raindrop?

A raindrop is a splinter of glass
Shimmering in the sunlight.

A raindrop is a silver fish
Sliding down the windowpane.

A raindrop is a silver petal
Falling off a flower.

A raindrop is an angel's halo
Glistening in the darkness.

A raindrop is a teardrop
Gliding down your face.

Chloe Smith (9)
Canon Maggs CE Junior School, Bedworth

What Is A Snowflake?

A snowflake is a silver pearl
Shining in the moonlight.

A snowflake is a spot of paint
Dancing through the air.

A snowflake is a tiny light
Glowing in the sunlight.

A snowflake is a flower
Floating round and round.

A snowflake is a silver coin
Gliding to the ground.

Charlotte Mallabone (9)
Canon Maggs CE Junior School, Bedworth

What Is A Cloud?

A cloud is a huge, juicy marshmallow
In lots of blue candy.

A cloud is pink candyfloss
Lying on a blue blanket.

A cloud is a big fluffy pillow
Lying on a big blue bed.

A cloud is a little bird's feather
Floating on blue water.

A cloud is a fluffy sheep
Standing in a field.

Connor Goold (9)
Canon Maggs CE Junior School, Bedworth

What Is A Cloud?

A cloud is feathery, white train steam
Drifting away in the wind.

A cloud is a pink candyfloss
Floating away in the deep ocean.

A cloud is a fluffy sheep
Sailing to a faraway land.

A cloud is a soft marshmallow
Disappearing into the distance.

A cloud is a squashy poodle's tail
Waggling along a long trip.

Ryan Allsopp (9)
Canon Maggs CE Junior School, Bedworth

What Is A Raindrop?

A raindrop is a bright red petal
Falling off a rose.

A raindrop is a glimmering bubble
Drifting through the sky.

A raindrop is a clear teardrop
Gliding down your cheek.

A raindrop is a diamond jewel
Shimmering round your neck.

A raindrop is a golden star
Sparkling in the moonlight.

Amie Johnson (9)
Canon Maggs CE Junior School, Bedworth

What Is A Cloud?

A cloud is a stray sheep
Wandering through a clear, blue pond.

A cloud is a piece of white candyfloss
Floating majestically through the silent air.

A cloud is a plush piece of wool
Sitting comfortably on a great blue sheet.

A cloud is an inaudible feather
Hovering briskly through the air.

A cloud is a smooth cushion
Relaxing on a sky-blue bed.

Daniel Cunnington (9)
Canon Maggs CE Junior School, Bedworth

What Is A Snowflake?

A snowflake is a fairy
Fluttering down to earth.

A snowflake is a diamond
Shining in a puddle of water.

A snowflake is a silver bead
Glistening on a sheet of silk.

A snowflake is a splinter of glass
Glinting in a beam of light.

A snowflake is a star
Twinkling like a cat's eye.

Shevonne Broadbent (9)
Canon Maggs CE Junior School, Bedworth

What Is A Raindrop?

A raindrop is like a splinter of shimmering glass
Falling through clouds.

A raindrop is like a glimmering, silver bead
Just landing in the fountain.

A raindrop is like a bubble, crystal clear
Floating down onto the dewy flowers.

A raindrop is like an angel's white wings
Fluttering down onto the snow-covered table.

A raindrop is like a silver star
Shining proudly in the sun.

Rachel Grant (9)
Canon Maggs CE Junior School, Bedworth

What Is A Snowflake?

A snowflake is an angel,
Falling gracefully down the horizon.

A snowflake is a fairy,
Fluttering smoothly down to the ground.

A snowflake is a piece of silk,
Smoothly covering the ground.

A snowflake is a silver bead,
Raining down on us.

A snowflake is a star,
Glittering through the land.

Toni Lovell (9)
Canon Maggs CE Junior School, Bedworth

What Is A Snowflake?

A snowflake is a bright, white light
Glittering as it falls onto the icy floor.

A snowflake is a piece of tinsel
Falling gracefully into the glistening trees.

A snowflake is a silver star
Gliding down from the sky.

A snowflake is a tiny, white bead
Spinning down into the glistening lake.

Olivia Fitz-James Johnson (9)
Canon Maggs CE Junior School, Bedworth

What Is A Cloud?

A cloud is a big chunk of candyfloss
Being eaten by a giant.

A cloud is some steam coming from a train
That toots a lot and likes animals.

A cloud is a shining, light feather
That is falling down from the beautiful Heaven above.

A cloud is a giant, delicious marshmallow floating down to earth
So everyone can go and take one bite each day till it's gone.

A cloud is a sheep who is being put into its pen
With all its friends and family.

Loic Wan (9)
Canon Maggs CE Junior School, Bedworth

What Is A Snowflake?

A snowflake is a silver piece of tinsel
Flying onto a Christmas tree.

A snowflake is a sparkling diamond
Floating to the ground.

A snowflake is an angel
Fluttering to the earth.

A snowflake is a shooting star
Flying over the houses.

A snowflake is a white butterfly
Falling to join its friends.

Laura Collins (9)
Canon Maggs CE Junior School, Bedworth

What Is A Raindrop?

A raindrop is a blue fish
Floating peacefully down to earth.

A raindrop is a piece of white glass
Falling down to earth silently.

A raindrop is a bubbly bubble
Sparkling from the blue sky.

A raindrop is an angel
Flying on top of a tree.

A raindrop is a swimming, blue fish
Swimming in the pond.

Katie-Ann Northall (9)
Canon Maggs CE Junior School, Bedworth

What Is A Cloud?

A cloud is a pure white puff of smoke
Falling down to earth.

A cloud is a gentle piece of candyfloss
Gliding down into my hand.

A cloud is a puff of train steam
Flying up into the sky.

A cloud is a heart shape
Obliterating my body.

A cloud is a feather
Floating down from Heaven.

Niall MacCallum (9)
Canon Maggs CE Junior School, Bedworth

What Is A Snowflake?

A snowflake is a pure white, silky dove
Drifting silently across blue, crystal-clear water.

A snowflake is like a crystal bead
Floating across the sky.

A snowflake is like a suede angel wing
Fluttering slowly down from Heaven.

A snowflake is like a bright, shining, silver sprinkle of light
Racing through thin air.

Joshua Loughrey (9)
Canon Maggs CE Junior School, Bedworth

A Yard Full Of Fun

A yard full of fun,
Fun for everyone.
As the teachers talk and the children laugh,
We all forget about the morning math.
As we eat our lunch,
With a munch and a crunch and some of us sneak to the bin,
We rush outside with a happy grin.
The toilets smell
And the yard is just swell
And we all have a lot to say,
But at the end of the day,
We must go away,
From a yard full of fun.

Shaun Donnelly (11)
Cathedral Primary School, Motherwell

My Boys

I have two cats, they are my boys.
They are both black, as black as night.
They run around, they jump and fight,
They jump on my bed, they give me a fright.
They are my boys, I love them lots,
Without them I would be lost.
They sleep most of the day
And they lie on your lap. Do they dream?
I do not know.
They chase their toys up and down,
Making a noise that annoys my mum.
They wake you up, a wet nose on your face
And still they wait till you get up.
They sit and stare till you give them a clap
And then they will go and have a nap.
They are my boys, I love them so,
Will I ever let them go?
That would have to be a really big *no!*

Lauren Thorburn (11)
Cathedral Primary School, Motherwell

Playtime

Playtime is a chance to play
A chance to run
A chance to make friends
A chance to have fun
But most of all it's a chance
You can make every day.

Fiona Ross (11)
Cathedral Primary School, Motherwell

Schooldays

I'm sleepy, cold and grumpy,
My body is tired and sore,
I can't believe the alarm's gone off
And it's Monday morning once more.

From downstairs I hear my mother call,
'Are you still in your bed?'
I shut my eyes and turn around
And pull my covers over my head.

Before I know I'm in at school,
All ready to start the day,
I settle down and listen
To all my teacher has to say.

She teaches maths and English,
She knows everything,
She draws and paints and sketches,
And even tries to sing.

She talks about some countries,
Some villages and towns,
She tells us about adjectives,
Adverbs and nouns.

She shows us a video
That was interesting to see,
She takes us to the gym hall,
For us to do PE.

I don't know where the day has gone,
It's already afternoon,
I really want to learn some more,
But home time comes too soon.

I quite enjoyed my day at school,
I never would have guessed,
I believe my mum when I hear her say,
'Your schooldays are the best.'

Shaun Nicholls (11)
Cathedral Primary School, Motherwell

My Fish

My fish is called Dory, she is very nosy.
She doesn't like swimming in dirty water,
But does tricks like Harry Potter.
She can be very noisy at times,
Flipping in the water, making lots of signs.
I don't know what I would do if she wasn't there,
I got Dory when I was nine years old.
Dory has a sign saying 'no swimming',
But that doesn't stop her.
My fish, Dory, is the eleventh fish I have had,
But she is not that bad.

Jordan Lewis (11)
Cathedral Primary School, Motherwell

Winter

Winter days, winter nights,
Snowflakes falling in the night.
The ground is cold, as cold as snow,
Igloos, snowmen, snow angels grow.
Kids are laughing, people snapping,
And hot chocolate is boiling.
Then comes summer, people smiling,
Pools are opening, birds singing
And daffodils blooming.

Adrian Pollock (11)
Cathedral Primary School, Motherwell

Blackpool

My holiday in Blackpool was amazing
Some sights made me stand gazing
Such as the Pleasure Beach
Which I thought out of reach

All of the rides were great
And I didn't stand around and wait
I went on the Irn-Bru Revolution, the Pepsi Max
And the Tango Ice Blast
They made my stomach churn and my heart burn

The restaurants were fantastic
The food had a delicious taste
And none of it ever went to waste

Another beautiful sight was the Blackpool Tower
It looked dashing at night with all its bright light
The walk of faith was very safe
Although we were all scared witless at the time

There was also a clown show
And the clown was called Mooky
He was very funny
And worked hard for his money

My week was over and I was homeward bound
I wasn't going back
(Well until next year that is)!

Jack Mullen (11)
Cathedral Primary School, Motherwell

School

I like school as I get to meet lots of different people
And I like doing school work.
I also like school as it lets me learn about all topics.
The best thing about school is making and meeting lots of friends.

Jodi Clinton (11)
Cathedral Primary School, Motherwell

Crazy Cats

I love cats because they're cute,
I love their coats and paws,
I love them when they play with me,
But I don't love their claws.

When my cat was a tiny kitten,
She used to run and hide,
Beneath the small space under the stairs
But now she is much too wide!

My cat looks like a little tiger
Except her coat is grey,
She likes to sleep on my bed,
She can sleep the day away.

My cat likes to climb up trees
And sleeps all tightly curled,
I love my cat very much,
I wouldn't change her for the world.

Lauren Bolton (11)
Cathedral Primary School, Motherwell

About Myself

I am very small
I like to play football
I like macaroni
And always wanted a pony
I never go to school
I'm always playing pool
I go to my granny's
And was taught never to be cruel
I love doing maths
And then I go in the bath
And then at night
I like to tuck up tight
And that's how I turned out to be.

Emma Young (11)
Cathedral Primary School, Motherwell

Summer

Summer is my favourite season,
It's warm and sometimes really hot.
On summer holidays you can go to the beach with your family
Or abroad to Spain, or even Hawaii.
Summer is the best season of the year,
You get to go out and play a lot,
Unlike winter when it's very cold and you are stuck in the house.

I love summer because it is a happy season
And the nights are shorter, which means more play for me.
Summer is not always a happy time for me,
Especially when I am stuck in a class doing work
And it's a really hot, hot day.
Summer, summer, summer, a happy kind of season.
I am very happy we get a season like summer.

Emmanuel Ndlovu (11)
Cathedral Primary School, Motherwell

Holidays

Holidays are fun, holidays are cool
Whenever we're on holiday, we're never at school
Every day we get a long lie, lazing around as the days go by
Watching television, this totally beats school
Eating junk food, it's better than cool!
You might go to Majorca or somewhere sunny
You might make a friend who will be really funny
Go to the beach or stay at the pool
But whatever you do, it will be mega cool!
Everybody knows all good things must come to an end
So say goodbye to your new, funny friend
Back home to Scotland to prepare for school
I can reassure you that won't be mega cool!

Lauren McShannon (11)
Cathedral Primary School, Motherwell

In The Playground

Silence, silence, silence all around
Silence is broken with the ringing of the bell.

No books, no pens, no papers, no rulers,
Just fun and games in the playground.

Balls, ropes and hula hoops
Is the lesson for us today.

In the playground sunny and bright,
Lots of children are playing and running about with delight.

Boys playing football, girls playing ropes,
Boys chasing girls with a kiss on a hope.

Toes out of school shoes, knees out of tights,
Rear ends out of trousers, just because of a fight.

The fight's all over as the janitor rings the bell,
A shake of a hand, we're all friends again,
Stand in line and off we go to class.

Sweet paper rustling, crisp bags blowing,
Silence returns to the playground once again.

Robyn Delaney (11)
Cathedral Primary School, Motherwell

Chocolate And Sweets

Chocolate and sweets are thoughts in my head,
Scrummy and creamy,
I'm in my bikini.
At the seaside, on a boat ride,
Licking my cone,
Talking on the phone,
These are thoughts in my head that cannot be read.

Adele Buchanan (11)
Cathedral Primary School, Motherwell

When I Grow Up

When I grow up
I want to be a teacher
A counsellor or a preacher
Or what about an astronaut who would travel to Mars
And see beyond the stars?

When I grow up
I want to be a superstar
Who would drive a sleek, black car
Or what about a wizard
Who could create a spell
For a horrible blizzard?

When I grow up
I want to be a famous actress
For all the world to see
Or what about an athlete
Who could win all the cups
And have blisters on her feet?

When I grow up
I want to be a TV presenter
I will present all the shows
Wearing high heels and having sore toes
Or what about a ballerina
I could dance and prance
And my name could be Cattrina?

Erin Eadie (11)
Cathedral Primary School, Motherwell

Seasons

I like summer 'cause it's sunny,
The nights are shorter
And I go outside to play with my friends.

But winter just drives me round the bend,
I hate it when it's cold and windy,
Just not the weather for me.

I get happy when spring comes along,
When all the birds sing their songs.
Summer and spring are my favourite seasons.

Last of all comes freezing autumn,
Where it's always dark and cold.
Though it isn't as bad as winter,
Autumn is really catchin' up,
Though it'll probably take a while,
'Cause winter's really rough.

Allan Hopkinson (11)
Cathedral Primary School, Motherwell

A Day At The Beach

I saw the blue sky was as shiny as a diamond,
The sand was as yellow as the sun,
The gulls flew over the bright sea screaming,
The people lay under the umbrellas
to shade them from the warm sun.
The clouds as fluffy as wool, high in the sky,
All the children making sandcastles in the sand.
I was crab fishing on the beach and I caught lots of crabs.
The sun was going down, it was time to go home.
I could smell my tasty tea.
I had a brilliant time at the beach.

Michael McCabe (11)
Cathedral Primary School, Motherwell

My Dog, Buster

M is for his messy and very muddy tricks
Y is for his youth

D is for his delighted face when I come home from school
O is for his orange ball which he always plays with
G is for the greatest dog ever

B is for his bulging, blue, puppy-dog eyes
U is for his unique size and shape
S is for his sky-high appetite
T is for his tiger-like teeth when seeing another dog
E is for his enormous amount of energy
R is for his roguishness when seeing food that is not being
                                             watched by anyone.

Natalie Thomson (11)
Cathedral Primary School, Motherwell

Playground Poets

Don't be bad to your dad,
Lend a pen to your friend,
Don't play hard in the yard,
Tell Mum what's in your tum,
See what you find and be kind,
Play gentle and don't go mental,
Share your sweets and your treats.

Megan Cook (11)
Cathedral Primary School, Motherwell

My Little Brother

My little brother used to be
A tiny bundle on my knee
Who fed and slept all through the day
But that's all changed I have to say

Our tidy home used to be
A place where you would come and see
Two quiet little girls play
But that's all changed I have to say

My father's car used to be
Clean and tidy, chocolate free
Where not a bit of rubbish lay
But that's all changed I have to say

My mum and dad used to be
Parents of only my sister and me
Who went to church and got peace to pray
But that's all changed I have to say

My life before used to be
As organised as ABC
But what a joy has come my way
I love him loads I have to say.

Katie Cunningham (11)
Cathedral Primary School, Motherwell

My Bike

My bike is fast
My bike is never last
It's not pink or blue
But the colour red would always do
The silver alloys go round and round
Not one bent spoke can be found
And when I'm bored I can go on the road because
My bike is fast and it's never last.

Anthony Maguire (10)
Cathedral Primary School, Motherwell

Whether The Weather

The sun, the rain
The clouds, the heat
The rainbows and the misty sleet
All sorts of weather can occur
From one minute to the next

Running down the street
Escaping from the rain
Sunshine comes from nowhere
Steam rises again

Lying in the garden
Relaxing in summer heat
Suddenly it's a downpour
And there's no one in the street

One day I'll live in a country
Where the weather is always fine
And I'll never need to worry
Whether it will be hail, rain or shine.

Lucy McCarron (11)
Cathedral Primary School, Motherwell

My Dog Poem

I've got a dog,
Her name is Molly,
Everyone thinks she is very jolly.

We take her for walks to the park
And when she plays with her ball,
She does very loud barks.

And sometimes when she is in her cage,
She pulls everything in and starts to chew it all.
But when she hears a phone call,
She starts to bark and play with her ball.

Lauren Carroll (10)
Cathedral Primary School, Motherwell

Marine Life

There are many creatures underwater,
From north, south, east and west.
Sharks are dangerous, seals are cute,
But to me dolphins are the best.

They come from different oceans,
Many kinds of fish.
Fishermen catch them in their nets,
To cook a delicious dish.

From the smallest creature in the water
To the largest in the land.
Hippos, crocodiles, penguins
And jellyfish on the sand.

Very few mammals,
Live in the water,
Including the whale, walrus,
Dolphin and otter.

The underwater world is very interesting,
All their different lives and ways,
Their hunting and eating habits,
The way they swim and play.

Nicole Leggate (11)
Cathedral Primary School, Motherwell

My Love

The heavenly person from above,
I love you, you sing like a dove,
Your eyes twinkle in the night,
I love you with all my might,
Tonight I have you in my sight,
My love, my love, my love.

Rachel Shields (10)
Cathedral Primary School, Motherwell

The Abandoned Dog

A little lost puppy alone in a sack
They abandoned her there and never looked back
She cried and she whimpered, that little black jewel
And wondered why humans were so very cruel

Tired and frightened she lay there all day
On the cold, hard ground as her life slipped away
No one to love her and give her a cuddle
Just dumped, like rubbish, right in a puddle

She was found by a worker the very next day
To the cat and dog home she was taken away
And that's where we found her, our little black loner
We needed a pet and she needed an owner

We call her Abbie, she is loyal and true
And we involve her in all that we do
She runs like a bullet right out of a gun
So full of mischief and so full of fun

But sometimes her eyes seem so far away
I wonder if she remembers that day
When the evil people left her for dead
All alone on the ground in a cold, damp bed

But then she perks up and barks over to me
And Abbie and I go for a walk before tea.

Rachel McCann (10)
Cathedral Primary School, Motherwell

My Rabbit, Angus

Rabbits are fluffy and puffy,
Some people call them bunnies.

My rabbit is called Angus,
He is black and white
And his eyes are very bright.

He lives in my home,
He likes to roam,
Sometimes he is full of fun
And likes to run.

He goes to sleep at night
And wakes up when it's light.

My mother is scared of Angus,
But my brother and I are not.
Angus is very funny
And he is the best bunny in the world.

Mhairi Duncan (11)
Cathedral Primary School, Motherwell

Horses, Horses, Horses!

I like horse riding quite a lot
My favourite speed is the trot
When I'm riding up and down
I soon lose my sad frown

If it's a stallion, foal or mare
They all move with such flair
On a strawberry roan, a breed so rare
At a gallop I feel the wind in my hair

Whether brown, chestnut or grey
They always seem to know the way
When I'm riding way up high
I see the countryside go by
The sky so blue, the grass so green
Nature is a beauty to be seen.

Colette Carr (10)
Cathedral Primary School, Motherwell

My Friend

She is small and black with eyes of green
That can be seen
Like shiny jewels in the moonlight beam.

For sixteen years she has lived in my house
And once I remember, she caught a mouse!

Sitting for hours on the garden fence,
Watching and waiting for who knows what,
Looking quite pleased with herself for what she has caught.

But now she is quite old and slow,
I am sure that all the birds and mice know
That Chloe is no longer able to hunt them for her dinner table!

Most days she can be seen
Fast asleep up on my bed,
All curled up and cosy,
Oh, how I love my cat called Chloe.

Aimee Flanagan (10)
Cathedral Primary School, Motherwell

Teighan

'Don't you touch me,' said the kid
For being just eight and very quick
And very old in things she did
But in others uneasy and sick.

She was edgy, disturbed and distressed
And yes she had a natural talent
In singing and dancing, was never depressed
But often lost in her surroundings.

I liked her a lot and she liked me
We learnt lots with each other
I taught her to live in a family
How it would be with a new mother.

Lauren McKinnon (10)
Cathedral Primary School, Motherwell

My Friends

M y friends are my own friends
Y ou all have friends too

F riends are there to comfort you
R eally, if you need them, they need you
I n happiness we share secrets
E very day we are there for each other
N ever will we accept an unhappy friend
D ay by day we are still best of friends
S leepovers and parties, make-up and clothes we are BFFL (best friends for life).

Kerry McDade (11)
Cathedral Primary School, Motherwell

Fairies

Fairies are magic and gentle to touch
But only special people can see them and bring them luck
They are so small you cannot find
Until you think hard and empty your mind
If you are feeling sad or feeling down
There will always be a fairy around
They leave coins for missing teeth
And sprinkle fairy dust underneath
If you are lucky you might see a fairy dance
Dreams and imagination can make you wary
But it's magic to be able to see a fairy.

Rachael Lamarra (10)
Cathedral Primary School, Motherwell

The Best Janny I Know

The best janny I know has got great jokes,
My janny likes a laugh when he's sweeping the path,
When he's picking up litter from the grass
And when he's cleaning up the class,
He always wants to have a laugh.

Sometimes he's cheery, sometimes he's mad
And he's yelling at the boys who've been bad.
Janny is helpful, janny is cheery,
He always makes everything oh so cleary.

If there is a floor that needs cleaning
Or a toilet needs fixing,
Janny will be there.
If there is a bin needs taking out,
Janny will be there as quick as a blink.

If there is a leak in the sink,
Or time to think,
Janny will be right there,
Just as he is here for us kids
At Cathedral Primary School.

Chloe Ruiz (10)
Cathedral Primary School, Motherwell

Family

F athers frighten you with ghastly smells that dwell in the bathroom
A nd your brother really annoys your mother
M others moan about their weight and looks
I f your sister's make-up isn't right, it always ends up in a fight
L ove your family like you love yourself, or your relationship will
  end up at the back of the shelf
Y ou should always love your family with all your might, or you
  could be grounded for more than a night.

Stefan Ward (10)
Cathedral Primary School, Motherwell

My Mum

My mum is a nurse
She has money in her purse
Because she works all day
She really deserves her pay

She weighs all the babies
And gives them their jabs too
She comes home and makes the dinner
For me and maybe even you!

I really love my mum
And in return she loves me too
I appreciate what she does for me
And I always will do!

Jessica O'Brien (10)
Cathedral Primary School, Motherwell

My Family

In my family there is my father, my brother
And most important of all, my mother
We are all very different in our own way
And we each like to have our say
My father and brother like football
But I would much rather go to the mall
My mother on the other hand
Thinks she can sing and would love to play in a band
I like to chat, dance and have fun
While my dad likes to be in the sun
There is one thing we all like to do
And that's to go on holiday and have lots of fun too.

Louise Murray (11)
Cathedral Primary School, Motherwell

The Wizard And The Owl

There once was a wizard
Who had a pointy hat,
His cloak was flat
As a worn-out mat.
The shapes on his cloak
Looked like a moon,
He brewed up his potions
With a cauldron and spoon.

His wand gave out
A bolt of lightning,
It struck his opponent
So hard it was frightening.
His owl chased his
Black, fat cat
And ate it all up
And that is that.

The wizard was in shock
With his hairy friend,
He turned him into
A nice whisky blend.
He took a quick sip
And that was the end.

Paul McGill (10)
Cathedral Primary School, Motherwell

Weather

When it is sunny
Everyone is happy
The birds are out
The children run about.

When it is windy
People are shivery
They stay in their houses
Quiet as mice.

When it is rainy
People are sad
They talk about the good weather they've had.

When it is snowy
People are cold
Children having snowball fights
On snowy nights.

I love the sun
But I have fun
In all weather.

Rebecca Fitzsimmons (10)
Cathedral Primary School, Motherwell

Ten Snowmen

Ten snowmen standing in a line
One fell down, then there were nine.

Nine snowmen, each had a mate
One got knocked down, then there were eight.

Eight snowmen all in Devon
One melted, then there were seven.

Seven snowmen with a pick 'n' mix
One got a sore tooth, then there were six.

Six snowmen did a skydive
One got lost, then there were five.

Five snowmen in a bore
One gave up, then there were four.

Four snowmen found a key
One was left out, then there were three.

Three snowmen all heard *boo*
One fell down, then there were two.

Two snowmen found a bun
One ran off, then there was one.

One snowman standing in the sun
He got too hot, then there was none!

Amy Stark (10)
Cathedral Primary School, Motherwell

Fitbaw, Fitbaw

Fitbaw, fitbaw
Whit a great game
Fitbaw, fitbaw
Av bin a fan since a was a wean
Fitbaw, fitbaw
Fir ninety minutes, whit exciting stuff
Fitbaw, fitbaw
Me, a jus canny git enough
Fitbaw, Fitbaw
I'd play all day
Fitbaw, fitbaw
A just kick the baw any old way
Fitbaw, fitbaw
Make me a star
Fitbaw, fitbaw
At home or afar.

Jordan Crisp (11)
Cathedral Primary School, Motherwell

Swish! Swish!

Here I am in the classroom,
But I cannot talk to you,
For the silence in this room
Would make a mouse's voice go boom!
My breathing is deep and full of fear.

I hear a cry and a swish or two,
I think about the poor soul who is on the other end,
Oh no! Peter is whispering again!

'Peter, go to the head,' *swish, swish*.
He comes back to the classroom looking in pain.
Home time, yes, no more daily pain,
Yes, it is the weekend, no more *swish, swish!*

Andrew Davis (11)
Charley Memorial Primary School, Belfast

My Birthday Party

Out of my window I see beggars,
Smoky skies and steam engines.
I go downstairs, see toys and clothes,
Maids working and family members coming.
I run and greet the family,
They're shouting, 'Where's the birthday girl?'

I smell coal, peat and smoke,
If it burns anymore I might choke.
We go into the dining room,
I see and smell food and drink.
I smell wine and water,
Meat and potatoes.

I sit down at my seat,
Family members around me.
We say our prayer,
We can now tuck in.
I eat my meat, potatoes and vegetables.

I hear everyone laughing,
Talking and crying.
I hear everyone sing.
When my cake is brought in,
I blow out my candles,
I make a wish.

I am able to play with my toys,
Friends and family.
I try on my clothes.
Yes! Everything fits!
I got a scarf and a pair of mittens.

Ami Thompson (10)
Charley Memorial Primary School, Belfast

An Ordinary Day

On the street I see matchmakers
They are shouting, 'Buy some handmade matches.'
From my bedroom I see people walk by
They look like rich teachers to me.

When I go out I smell fumes
Horrible fumes from the factories
Mother's perfume brings me warmth
In the house our lovely smelling flowers bloom.

I taste my delicious meals at night
I taste my warm drinks
I taste them dawn to dusk
Inside my house that brings me warmth.

From the door I hear the rain
From the window I hear shouting
From my room I hear laughter
From the house I hear singing.

In the cupboard I touch glass
I also touch silverware
All this brings love to my heart
In my own family.

In my wardrobe I feel clean clothes
In my living room I feel the hot fire
Inside myself I feel my heart pounding
All this goes on inside my warm and loving house.

I see the maids at work
Milking the cows as their morning job
Doing jobs for Mother and Father
Buying presents for my birthday!

Emma Thompson (10)
Charley Memorial Primary School, Belfast

All Alone

I heard the clip-clop of the horses' hooves
As they pulled the cart down the street.
I saw the poor people
Curling down on the hard stones trying to sleep.
But as I heard the singing of the rich people in the house behind me,
My heartbeat slowed down.
Suddenly I felt cold,
I would never be there,
I would never have happiness again.
But a wealthy man approached me,
He threw me some money then he walked away.
I was so grateful,
My heart sang out in joy.
The factory smoke choked me,
But I didn't care.
As I looked in the house again,
I saw myself knocking at the door.
Somebody opened it,
I felt warmness as I had never felt before,
But I was still lying on the street.

Anne Henderson (9)
Charley Memorial Primary School, Belfast

The Starving Boy At The Train Station

I'm sitting on my own, nothing to do, no one to talk to,
Starvation's starting to come to me.
I hear the sound, *bang, bang, bang!*
When the train is coming to a halt.
I feel the pain of people kicking me on the way past,
No one will give me money.
Every day I see the rotting food
And see other people throwing food and paper down.
I dash across the stony ground to grab the leftovers.

Christopher Cullen (10)
Charley Memorial Primary School, Belfast

Victorian Game

I am running down the lane
To get to my party early.
Stop! What's this?

I think it is a gold coin.
I'd better pick it up,
It's nice and shiny.

It smells like new.
That's probably why it looks
So nice and shiny.

I'd better run fast,
My very own party
Is about to start.

I'm nearly there!
Wait, there's no cars
At my big house.

That game was fun
Oh, I really wish I had
That nice, shiny gold coin.

Adam Gorringe (8)
Charley Memorial Primary School, Belfast

A Kennings Poem

A fox:
Fierce fighter
Night lighter
Scramming scratcher
Prowling, growling
Rabbit hunter
Spectacular hunter
Twinkling eyes.

Lauren Galliford (8)
Coed Glas Primary School, Llanishen

Do You Know Who I Am?

Blue skin,
Bad grin,
Eat food,
In mood,
Big eyes,
Never cries,
Have wheels,
Big deals,
White hat,
Am fat,
Have goggles,
Mind boggles,
Have a song,
Never wrong.

I'm the Crazy Frog!

Ryan Moore (8)
Coed Glas Primary School, Llanishen

Guess Who I Am

Weary face
Round eyes
Wet nose
Cute paws
Fluffy fur
Smooth head
Guess who I am.

Meg Owen (8)
Coed Glas Primary School, Llanishen

Rider!

I used to be a rider,
But now I'm a jockey.
I used to ride through the cool breeze,
But now I'm in the Kentucky Derby.
I'm riding, riding, riding,
Faster and faster and faster.
I used to be a quarter of the way through the race,
But now I'm halfway.
I'm coming from behind the person in front,
But now I'm in front of him.
I used to be last,
But now I'm first.
I used to be a rider,
But now I'm a winner!

Natalie Vaughan (10)
Coed Glas Primary School, Llanishen

Child Of The Week

Monday's child stays in bed
Tuesday's child is always fed
Wednesday's child is lazy too
Thursday's child won't go to the loo
Friday's child screams and screams
Saturday's child dreams of creams
And the child that is born on the Sabbath Day,
Always tells me to play.

Charlea Heathfield-Eades (8)
Coed Glas Primary School, Llanishen

What Am I?

Little squealer
Fast scrammer
Fish eater
Green eyes
Fat tummy
Cute loving
I am a kitten.

Bethan John (8)
Coed Glas Primary School, Llanishen

A Rocket

Fierce flyer
Flying fantasy
Speedy mover
Fire blaster
Tall machine.

George Davies (8)
Coed Glas Primary School, Llanishen

An F1 Car

Scary sound
Strange looks
Quick turning
Sweaty people
Good winners.

Steffan Hugh Davies (9)
Coed Glas Primary School, Llanishen

The Day The Zoo Escaped

The day the zoo escaped
The monkeys swung out happily
The spiders crawled out nervously
The tigers charged out poshly
The rabbits hopped out proudly
But the sleepy sloth
Just hung around.

William Mesoud (8)
Coed Glas Primary School, Llanishen

The Day The Zoo Escaped!

The monkeys rushed out happily
The spiders crawled out quietly
The tigers leapt out joyfully
The rabbit hopped out funnily

But the sleepy sloth
Just hung around.

Mawgan Newman (8)
Coed Glas Primary School, Llanishen

The Day The Zoo Escaped

The monkeys swung out happily
The spiders crawled out quietly
The tigers marched out proudly
The rabbits hopped out loudly
But the hippopotamus sleepily
Just hung around.

Lewis Prole (8)
Coed Glas Primary School, Llanishen

A Kennings Poem

Black mister
Red eyes
Frightening surpriser
Poisonous looker
Bobbing tentacles
Rough skin
Who am I?

Freya Cuthbert (8)
Coed Glas Primary School, Llanishen

A Panda

Lazy mover
Black paws
Fast muncher
Bamboo eater
Glowing eyes
Huge surprise.

Kirsty Williams (8)
Coed Glas Primary School, Llanishen

What Am I?

Spotty skin,
Happy grin,
Long neck,
Smiling mouth,
Munching noise,
Crunching leaves.

It is a giraffe!

Laura Mulder (8)
Coed Glas Primary School, Llanishen

The Day The Zoo Escaped

The monkeys snuck out happily
The spiders crawled out anxiously
The tigers charged out proudly
The rabbits rushed out joyfully
But the sad hippopotamus
Just sat on his own.

Joseph Price (8)
Coed Glas Primary School, Llanishen

A Kennings Poem

Rumbling monster
Fast sprinter
Races well
Handles well
Road legal.

Taylor Brown (8)
Coed Glas Primary School, Llanishen

It's Lovely

Dancing dasher
Elegant mover
Pretty tail
Beautiful blue
Don't forget
They are so lovely.

Joanne Chandler (8)
Coed Glas Primary School, Llanishen

Blazing Inferno

I used to be destructive
But now I am peaceful

I used to be raging
But now I am waiting

I used to think I was invincible
But now I know that I was wrong

I used to be a killer
But now I am dead

I used to be a blazing inferno
But now I am a pile of ashes.

Brendan Kearon (10)
Coed Glas Primary School, Llanishen

The Days Of The Week Poem

Monday's child stays in bed
Tuesday's child is not fed
Wednesday's child is lazy too
Thursday's child stays on the loo
Friday's child screams and screams
Saturday's child is full of dreams
But the child that is born on the Sabbath day
Is ready to play.

Celyn Keene-Proctor (8)
Coed Glas Primary School, Llanishen

Sunset

Sunset
Delightful, pleasing
Glistening and shimmering
Amazing, calming, beautiful, relaxing
Day's end.

Molly Proudman (11)
Coed Glas Primary School, Llanishen

I Used To Be . . .

I used to fall off stabilisers,
But now I glide on two wheels.
I used to play in a paddling pool,
But now I swim in the lanes.
I used to struggle with my ABCs,
But now I write stories.
I used to think that I could fly,
But now I know that this is impossible.
I used to wear booties,
But now I wear shoes.

I used to use poppers,
But now I use buttons.
I used to say 'Mama' and 'Dada',
But now I say 'Mum' and 'Dad'.
I used to use crayons,
But now I use pens.
I used to find 2+2 hard,
But now I square numbers.
I used to have a nightlight,
But now I sleep in the dark.

Bethan Jenkins (10)
Coed Glas Primary School, Llanishen

Friends

Friends
Kind and caring
By your side
Happy, joyful, cheerful, glad
Loyal.

Danielle Thwaites (10)
Coed Glas Primary School, Llanishen

I Used To Be . . .

I used to be a seed,
But now I am a leaf.
I used to be a caterpillar,
But now I am a cocoon.
I used to be the sea,
But now I am the clouds.

I used to believe in fairies,
But now I know they're not real.
I used to be an angel,
But now I am a devil.
I used to be a shy person,
But now I am confident.
I used to believe that war would end,
But now I know that won't happen.

Lauren Hyde (11)
Coed Glas Primary School, Llanishen

The Week's Children

Monday's child stays in bed,
Tuesday's child has lost his head.
Wednesday's child is lazy too,
Thursday's child is kept in the zoo.
Friday's child screams and screams,
Saturday's child loves ice creams.
But the child that is born on the Sabbath day,
Is caring and loving till the end of the day.

George Carson (9)
Coed Glas Primary School, Llanishen

I Used To . . .

I used to be a toddler,
But now I'm a child.
I used to be a seed,
But now I'm a flower.
I used to believe in Father Christmas,
But now I don't.
I used to play with Barbie dolls,
But now I play with computer games.
I used to have a bottle,
But now I have a glass.
I used to be afraid,
But now I have no fear.

I used to have a crib,
But now I have a bed.
I used to be a twig,
But now I am a branch.
I used to play the guitar,
But now I play the violin.

Jessica Dyer (10)
Coed Glas Primary School, Llanishen

What Day Were You Born On?

Monday's child stays in bed,
Tuesday's child has a big fat head.
Wednesday's child is lazy too,
Thursday's child loves the zoo.
Friday's child screams and screams,
Saturday's child shouts for ice creams.
But the child that is born on the Sabbath day,
Sings and sings until the end of the day.

Kia Shah (8)
Coed Glas Primary School, Llanishen

I Used To Be . . .

I used to want the best Barbie doll,
But now I don't have time.
I used to fly my own plane,
But now it's run out of fuel.

I used to think that life was a game to play,
But now I know reality.
I used to always wish for peace,
But now it seems far away.

I used to be very much adored,
But now I'm just not trusted.
I used to have an angelic smile,
But now that smile's faded.
I wished a lot of things,
But now I have a goal.

Sian Ellis (10)
Coed Glas Primary School, Llanishen

I Used To Be . . .

I used to be a caterpillar,
But now I'm a butterfly.
I used to be afraid,
But now I'm confident.
I used to be a flat balloon,
But now I soar above the clouds.

I used to believe in Father Christmas,
But now I know it's not true.
I used to be an angel,
But now I'm a devil.
I used to be a spine,
But now I'm a book.

Sophie Rooke (11)
Coed Glas Primary School, Llanishen

Bedroom

The door squeals as its delicate body is bent back and forth.
The raging carpet cries as its short hair is trampled on by elephants.
The tiresome bed opens its mouth for its dinner and closes it
                                                  when asleep.
The plants smile as their long arms reach out to the light and the
                                                  buds' eyes open.

The angry wardrobe's bones rattle as a pack of wolves enter,
The books on the shelf grumble, waiting for their teeth to be cleaned.
The Lego roars as the pieces are pushed together and soon have
                                                  bumps on their head.
The ticking clock slowly moves its hands, trying to catch its prey.

Christine Grimes (10)
Coed Glas Primary School, Llanishen

Bedroom

The bed curls up and starts to sleep
Teddies join paws and sing joyfully
The floor shakes off all the rubbish with anger
TV wakes up to see the room chaotic and cluttered

The CD player sings of happiness filling the room with joy
The nightie dances around the floor
Cake, half-eaten, starts to chatter
Blu-tack jumping off the wall onto a teddie-filled bed.

Jessica Williams (11)
Coed Glas Primary School, Llanishen

Bedroom

The door stands guard over my private domain,
Never falling, never giving way.
The bed hugs me to sleep each night,
Sending me hurtling into a world of fantasy.
The orang-utan swings acrobatically on the agitated lamp,
Wondering if he'll ever escape to freedom.
Robots look longingly from the window sill
At the ground far below in the depth of dying toys.

The drawers hold the heavy burden of clothes in its many arms,
But supporting it without fail.
The PS2 games whinge and whine
When they are not taken to their mother.
Books shuffle impatiently as they wait for someone to open them,
So they can teach all they know.
The mirror screams in horror
As a strange, two-legged monster looks into it.

Daniel Bardsley (10)
Coed Glas Primary School, Llanishen

Bedroom

Stiff door's feet tickle as they brush the carpet's soft fingers.
Bed's baggy duvet, baggy cushion hair,
Cushions big and plump from eating too much stuffing.
The desk's drawers are its thousand mouths.
Bottle cap's stiff eyes shining.
Lamp setting off a grenade, causing a blinding light.
Cardiff Blues' big bear watching over my possessions.
Magazines gossiping all the time.
Bin mouth wide open, gobbling up all the garbage.

Morgan Church (11)
Coed Glas Primary School, Llanishen

I Used To Be . . .

I used to be wild and crazy,
But now I am much calmer.
I used to want everything I saw,
But now I understand how much items cost.
I used to play all day,
But now I have a rest.

I used to be afraid and little,
But now I fear nothing.
I used to smile all day,
But now it has started to fade.
I used to need my mummy to guide me everywhere,
But now I lead myself.

Megan Chisholm-Jones (10)
Coed Glas Primary School, Llanishen

I Used To Be . . .

I used to be a unit,
But now I'm ten.
I used to crawl when I was a baby,
But now I walk.
I used to think monsters were real,
But now I know they're not.

I used to be a small fish in a big pond,
But now I am a big fish in a small pond.
I used to watch CBBC,
But now I watch Eastenders and Coronation Street.

Nicole Hicks (10)
Coed Glas Primary School, Llanishen

I Used To Dream . . .

I used to dream of feeding myself,
But now my dream's come true.
I used to think life was easy,
But now I know it's a challenge.
I used to play with Action Man,
But now I'm scoring goals.

I used to be shy and embarrassed if a child laughed at me,
But now I ignore them and walk away.
I used to get tired easily,
But now I can run forever.
I used to have teddies to cuddle at night,
But now there's not a single one in sight.

Thomas Pine (10)
Coed Glas Primary School, Llanishen

The Poem To Win

Monday's child stays in bed,
Tuesday's child is not fed.
Wednesday's child is lazy too,
Thursday's child goes to the loo.
Friday's child likes to scream,
Saturday's child likes ice creams.
And the child that is born on the Sabbath day,
Is bright and kind and ready to play.

Daryl Mackay (8)
Coed Glas Primary School, Llanishen

I Used To Be . . .

I used to be a twig,
But now I'm a branch.
I used to be a seed,
But now I'm a flower.
I used to play with Barbies,
But now I play with my PlayStation.
I used to have a cot,
But now I have a bed.
I used to play the recorder,
But now I play the violin.
I used to be a caterpillar,
But now I am a butterfly.
I used to be a magnet,
But now I am a fly.
I used to be afraid,
But now I am more confident.

Sophia Ouaaziz (10)
Coed Glas Primary School, Llanishen

I Used To Be . . .

I used to be a root,
But now I'm starting to grow.
I used to cry,
But now I don't cry as much.
I used to be a naïve and silly,
But now I'm more sensible.

I used to be a seed,
But now I am a sapling.
I used to have no confidence,
But now I shine.

Danielle O'Brien (10)
Coed Glas Primary School, Llanishen

The Goblin's Poem

Scuttling, running, Goblin Hut in amongst the green branch trees,
Scowling, prowling Goblin Hut, eighteen years and nineteen days,
Scowling, prowling, scuttling quick to the Goblin Hut,
Work at the Goblin Hut!
Nineteen years, nineteen days, a year aged and nothing's changed,
Running, jumping, heaving, levering,
Every goblin's here at the Goblin Hut!
But the fun ends here at night!
Everything's still, everything's quiet,
Shh! Sleeping goblins at the Goblin Hut.

Natalie Lloyd-Gale (8)
Coed Glas Primary School, Llanishen

Bird

I used to be an egg sitting in a bundle of sticks and straw,
Now I am a tiny chick learning to fly.
I used to be a tiny chick learning to fly,
Now I am a beautiful bird flying high amongst colossal trees.
I used to be a beautiful bird flying high in the sky,
Now I am an old, frail bird nesting in a bed of sticks.
I used to be an old, frail bird nesting in a bed of sticks,
Now I am a helpless feather drifting down from an empty nest.

Kirsty O'Donnell (10)
Coed Glas Primary School, Llanishen

I Used To Be . . .

I used to be unhappy,
But now I am content.
I used to be an empty seed,
But now I am an open book.
I used to always get things wrong,
But now I feel confident.
I used to crawl,
But now I walk like an adult.

Jodie Welsh (10)
Coed Glas Primary School, Llanishen

I Used To Be . . .

I used to be a bud,
But now I am a rose.
I used to be shy,
But now I am confident.
I used to love to make a noise,
But now I desire peace and quiet.

Katie Nash (11)
Coed Glas Primary School, Llanishen

Mr Hall

There was a man called Mr Hall,
Who went to take a call.
He ran away the very same day,
Never came back at all.

Jaimie-Lee O'Shea (11)
Coed Glas Primary School, Llanishen

The Rumbly Rumbler

It's a rumbling monster,
It's fast with fast wheels,
Big tyres,
Scary lights, so big they even look like traffic lights,
They're so big,
Heavy moves too.

Sophie Wall (8)
Coed Glas Primary School, Llanishen

The Day The Zoo Escaped

The monkeys rushed out cheekily,
The spiders crawled out shyly,
The tigers rushed out happily,
The rabbits hopped out quietly,
But the sloth, sleepy, just hung around.

Angharad Brown (8)
Coed Glas Primary School, Llanishen

Dan In A Can

There once was a boy called Dan,
Who lived with a drink in a can.
But against his luck,
Someone drank him up
And now he lives inside that man.

Samuel Tuson (11)
Coed Glas Primary School, Llanishen

Rainbow - Cinquain

Rainbow,
Amazing sight,
Good shape, red and yellow,
Happy, joyful, lonely and warm,
Rainbow.

Sophie Eddy (10)
Coed Glas Primary School, Llanishen

My Dad's Wedding

My dad's wedding,
Exciting and tearful,
Enjoying, eating and dancing,
Delighted to be there,
A great day.

Ashleigh Williams (10)
Coed Glas Primary School, Llanishen

Family

Family,
Brothers, sisters,
Annoying, bratty, fun,
We're one big family,
Together.

Josie Dunne (10)
Coed Glas Primary School, Llanishen

I Live In Fear

I used to live in happiness,
In a beautiful, colossal house,
But now I live in fear,
In a small, puny cottage with a red cross on the door.

I used to be a young, lively child,
But now I'm a young, terrified child,
Cooped up and shy.

I used to think there was no such thing as sadness,
But now I think there is no such thing as happiness.

Annalise Daly (10)
Coed Glas Primary School, Llanishen

I Used To Fear

I used to be kind,
But now I rob banks.
I used to be wanted for kindness,
But now I am wanted for murder.
I used to be caring,
But now I am careless.
I used to fear,
But now I live the fear.

Georgina Mathlin (10)
Coed Glas Primary School, Llanishen

World War II

World War II,
Danger and shooting,
Killing and devastation,
Unhappiness, misery and heartbreak,
Fighting.

Daniel Heathfield-Eades (11)
Coed Glas Primary School, Llanishen

My Mysterious Bedroom

The bed rumbles as the wise sleepers
Experience happy dreams.

The stuffed toys sit crammed up in the corner
Thinking gloomy thoughts.

Drawers clatter as they whizz open
And slam shut non-stop.

The dancing lamp flickers
Until its magical light fades away.

Hannah Jowett (10)
Coed Glas Primary School, Llanishen

Cyril The Squirrel

There was once a young man called Cyril,
Who actually came from the Wirral.
He sprang from some weeds
And ate nuts and seeds,
So the neighbours all called him a squirrel!

Josh Woods (10)
Coed Glas Primary School, Llanishen

Mr Hall

There once was a teacher called Mr Hall,
He taught in Coed Glas one and all,
He shaved off his hair,
But he didn't care,
Even though it made him look small.

Emily Jones (11)
Coed Glas Primary School, Llanishen

My Poem About How I Feel

I feel happy when I go to my cousin's house.
I feel horrible when I get the blame.
I feel dull when I go to the hospital.
I feel angry when I get bullied.
I feel brilliant if I cut a cake.
I feel complicated when I do my homework.
I feel bored when I work hard.
I feel stupid when I lose something precious.
I feel excited in Eid.
I feel fantastic when I go on a trip.
I feel clumsy when I miss something exciting.
I feel cheerful when I have sweets.
I feel good-humoured if I do PE.
I feel bad when I get told off.
I feel sad when people talk about death.
I feel frustrated when I have to do things at the same time.

Taslima Akther (9)
Culloden Primary School, London

My Poem About How I Feel

I feel jolly when I play my Game Boy
And unhappy when I come to school.
I feel bored when I have to read a book,
And happy when it's playtime.
I feel pleased when I find my work right,
And glad when I go on the computer.
I feel delighted when I play football in PE
And angry when someone bullies me.
I feel excited when I have a gift,
And cheerful when I do a score in PE.
I feel thankful when my brother gives me a gift,
And joyful when I watch football.

Imran Hussain (10)
Culloden Primary School, London

My Poem About How I Feel

I feel happy when I play outside,
And sad when we don't go swimming.
I feel annoyed when we play cricket,
And pleased when we play basketball.
I feel disappointed when we do science,
And happy when we do literacy.
I feel unhappy when I get sick,
And delighted when I go to the funfair,
And awful when my sister cries.
I feel cheerful when I go to the beach,
And troubled when I get told off.
I feel excited at the shopping centre,
And downhearted when I go to school.
I feel bored when I do geography,
And merry when we go swimming.
I feel gloomy when we go on boring trips,
And lively when it's sunny.
I feel depressed when it is raining,
And excited when we do golden time.

Dalena Dang (9)
Culloden Primary School, London

My Poem About How I Feel

I feel ashamed when I'm told off,
I feel downhearted when someone passes away.
I feel sleepy in school,
I like sleeping.
I feel shocked when I go somewhere,
I'm glad when I go swimming,
I'm sad when I get out of swimming,
I get bored when my mum sees her friend
I like playing football.

Ajwad Ahmed (9)
Culloden Primary School, London

My Poem About How I Feel

I feel happy when I go shopping with my mum,
And sad when my mum's not at home.

I feel excited when it's nearly the six week holiday,
And miserable when I fall down.

I feel annoyed when I play basketball,
Also disappointed when I don't have friends.

I feel unhappy when teachers look at me,
And lively when I go to the funfair.

I feel jolly when I go to school,
And merry when someone tells me a joke.

I feel pleased when we go on a fun trip,
Also delighted when I sleep over at my cousin's.

I feel hungry when I travel,
And hate it when I have to wake up to go to the toilet.

I feel angry when people cuss my friends
Also tired when I have to wake up for school.

I feel super when I have a party,
And bored at home.

I feel dizzy, when I turn around
Also upset when people die.
I feel gloomy when I'm ill.

That's how I feel.

Randa Hassan (9)
Culloden Primary School, London

My Poem About How I Feel

I feel very miserable when I go the Idea Store, sitting there bored,
And sad when my dad hits my baby sister.
I feel so excited when I am in my aunt's house,
And especially very pleased when I get to go to the funfair.
I feel very annoyed when I play cricket,
And really jolly when I watch football.
I feel so angry when my little brother bites me,
And very lively when we get to go to a fun trip.
I feel really delighted when I get to go to the beach
And so, so, so gloomy when I don't have anything I want.
I feel cross when I do history,
And very glad when I go for a nice walk.
I feel really grateful when I see my cousin coming to our house.

Soumayah Chakir (9)
Culloden Primary School, London

My Poem About How I Feel

I like running on a sunny day
And moaning when I get hay fever
I feel grateful on Wednesday because of swimming
And happy when I go to bed.
I feel astonished when I get caught doing something wrong,
And smart when I get all my questions right.
I feel amazed when my sister listens to me,
And slow when I finish my work last.
I feel mean when I shout at my sister,
And I feel stupid when I cry.
I feel lame when I say something that is really old
And feel crazy when I let my hair out.
I feel bad when I get angry
And I feel grateful when I get presents.

Valerie Bensalem (9)
Culloden Primary School, London

My Poem About How I Feel

I feel happy when I go on holidays,
And feel annoyed when I am ill.

I am pleased when I have baby brothers and sisters,
And bored when people come to my house.

I am sad when it is sunny,
And love it when it rains.

I feel angry when my brother hits me
And feel lovely when I go swimming.

I hate it when my sister wakes me up,
And unhappy when I have to do my homework.

I go mad to come to school,
And funny when people make sad faces.

Tanjima Khanam (9)
Culloden Primary School, London

My Poem About How I Feel

I like playing sports like cricket, hockey and basketball,
And I enjoy playing PS2
I hate it when it rains,
And I'm happy when it's sunny.
I feel super when I'm swimming,
And angry when people cuss me.
I feel famished when I'm fasting,
And tired when I wake up.
I feel miserable when someone dies,
And happy when I juggle.
I feel bad when I'm in trouble,
And I feel dumb when I do something stupid.

Jamal Uddin (9)
Culloden Primary School, London

My Poem About How I Feel

I feel pleased when I play outside.
I feel excited when Liverpool play Fulham.
I feel happy when I clock a game.
I feel surprised when I go on holiday.
I feel sad when people cuss me.
I enjoy playing wrestling.
I feel dizzy when I spin around.
I feel angry when I beat someone up.
I feel furious when someone throws something on me.

Shipu Alom (9)
Culloden Primary School, London

My Poem About How I Feel

I feel cheerful when I'm at Chelmsford,
I feel gloomy when I'm at home.
I feel excited all about Eid,
I feel downhearted when it's not Eid.
I feel pleased that I'm not a boy,
I feel annoyed when I get something wrong.
I feel thankful if I get a gift from someone,
And unhappy when someone dies.
I feel merry when I play with my friends,
But upset when I'm alone.
I feel bright when Shania sends me cards,
But disappointed if she doesn't phone me.

Sahidah Shahrazad (10)
Culloden Primary School, London

My Poem About How I Feel

I feel happy on a Wednesday
And sad on a Monday
Because I have to do lots of work,
And I like Wednesdays because I get to go swimming,
And sometimes we get to play in the water.
I feel cross when I have to do lots of writing,
And unhappy when I don't get to go swimming.
I hate it when I can't be a team captain,
And happy when people make me laugh.
My favourite sport is basketball and tennis.
I like playing pool and like doing art.

Chantelle da Silva (9)
Culloden Primary School, London

My Poem About How I Feel

I get miserable when I get told off,
And I was excited when Real Madrid won against Real Betis.
I was sad when Real Madrid lost against Lyon,
And I'm unhappy when my mum hits me.
I like chocolate mousse and ice cream,
And I'm happy when I play Smackdown Vs Rau and Fifa '0b.
I get annoyed when my mum watches Indian films
I felt shocked when Thierry Henry scored that beautiful goal.

Tofayel Ahmad Choudrey (9)
Culloden Primary School, London

My Poem

I am happy when I go swimming to splash around
I am sad when I have to wake up for school
I am pleased when I have to go to my nan's house
I like riding my bike
I feel down-hearted when Hollie cusses me
I am happy when I wake puppies.

Connor Smith (9)
Culloden Primary School, London

Autumn - Haikus

Red and gold and brown
Autumn colours falling down
Crunchy, crispy leaves.

Hallowe'en is here
Flapping capes and ghostly-masks
Noises fill the air

Boom, bang, crash, whizz, whee!
Flying colours everywhere
Firework night is here.

Ripe seeds fill the trees
Mahogany conkers fall
Squirrels hide away

The trees lose their leaves
Cold frost covers the hard ground
Autumn is over.

Jacqueline Baker (11)
Darvel Primary School, Darvel

Autumn Celebrations! - Haikus

It is autumn now
Golden leaves fall from the trees
Bedding on the ground.

It is Hallowe'en
Children wearing scary masks
Sweets clasped in their hands.

It is Bonfire Night
Fireworks go off in the air
Sitting by the fire.

It is winter now
I miss autumn now it's gone
Waiting till next year!

Erin Provan (10)
Darvel Primary School, Darvel

Autumn - Haikus

People falling down
As the leaves are soggy wet,
Really squelchy grass!

Big bangs and big booms
Fireworks fly over our heads
Going up then bang!

The foxes rustle
As the rushing conkers fall
Ready for sleeping!

It is Hallowe'en
Round the doors to get some sweets
I am Frankenstein!

James Watt (11)
Darvel Primary School, Darvel

Autumn - Haikus

Welcome to autumn
Crispy leaves are falling down
Darkness over sky.

Witches everywhere
Hallowe'en is nearly here
What are you wearing?

Firework night is here
Fireworks for Guy Fawkes' night, bang
Loud noise everywhere.

All the lovely leaves
Blow away in the strong wind
Bye bye little leaves.

Jennifer Paterson (11)
Darvel Primary School, Darvel

Autumn - Haikus

Crispy, crunchy leaves
Rustle while they all fall down
Gold ones are the best!

Hallowe'en is great!
Come along and you will see
You get sweets and crisps

Fireworks are good fun
Fireworks happen once a year
Try or regret it.

All I am saying
Is that autumn is the best
Of all the seasons.

Sorcha Johnstone (11)
Darvel Primary School, Darvel

Autumn - Haikus

Rustling through the leaves,
On a lovely autumn day,
Leaves fall everywhere.

Hallowe'en has come
People are wearing costumes,
Big bags full of sweets.

Here come the fireworks,
They are all kinds of colours,
Bang, clatter, boom, crash!

Now comes the winter,
All of the leaves have fallen,
Snow is everywhere.

Alice Boyd (10)
Darvel Primary School, Darvel

Autumn Leaves - Haikus

Trees are getting bare,
Leaves are crispy on the ground,
As people walk past.

In the woods with trees,
The leaves are changing colour,
As people walk past.

Hallowe'en is here,
Children go for trick or treat,
In the autumn time.

Now it's Bonfire Night,
Bang, bang, boom go the fireworks,
In the autumn time.

Devlin Greig (11)
Darvel Primary School, Darvel

Autumn - Haikus

Autumn is here now!
Leaves fall gently and rustle.
Bonfire Night is soon.

Wet rain in morning,
Crispy, golden leaves on path.
Hallowe'en is here!

Kids dress as monsters
Pumpkins on sale at Asda.
Witches haunt the streets.

Cold mornings are here.
Hats, gloves and scarves are worn now
Wet webs in morning.

Sarah Murray (11)
Darvel Primary School, Darvel

Autumn - Haikus

Leaves gold and yellow
Fall all of the time like stars
From the sky at night.

It comes once a year
Gives someone a great big fright
It is Hallowe'en!

Flying everywhere
Blowing up in the air cool
Colours are wicked

We battle with them
We look for them on the ground
Green and brown conkers.

Andrew Hyslop (11)
Darvel Primary School, Darvel

Autumn - Haikus

Here comes the autumn
The final season this year
A new year is near.

Gold, brown and red leaves
Scattered on the crunching ground
The trees are left bare.

Hallowe'en has come
Aliens, ghouls and monsters
Out to get some sweets.

Bonfire Night is here
Guy Fawkes is ablaze tonight
Fireworks loud and bright.

Scott Elder (11)
Darvel Primary School, Darvel

The Autumn Rose - Haikus

The blood-red rose stands,
Preparing for the winter,
And its snowy wall.

In the green grass field,
It stands all alone again,
Awaiting its death.

But every summer,
It grows again, blossoming,
As the sun beats down.

During this autumn,
It glows along with the leaves,
Which are gold once more.

When the red rose dies,
It dies with an autumn sight,
Which is beautiful.

Sean Hunter (11)
Darvel Primary School, Darvel

Autumn - Haikus

Leaves rustle and fall
As autumn is coming now
Fireworks go boom bang.

Bonfire night will come
Crispy leaves will fall from trees
Fireworks go boom, bang!

Green grass stops growing
Umbrellas will go up now
Leaves will fall on me.

Bright orange and red
Conkers lying on the ground
Leaves lie all day long.

Gemma Yeudall (11)
Darvel Primary School, Darvel

Nature's Words

Rushing out of my classroom door
I hear the screams and shouts like a distant dream
Cars rushing by like a tornado
Little children play on their bicycles
Pedalling around and around
Birds chirping in the distance
The cold air bristling on me like snowflakes.

Shhh!

The whistle blows
Stand still
And back I go to my class
Goodbye noises come and go again.

Isabella Kowalski (9)
Eastbury Farm JMI & Nursery School, Northwood

The Delicate Leaves

Leaves float down slowly doing flips in the air,
As light as a feather,
Going down, down, down,
Crunching as I walk on them,
Sounding like someone eating crackers,
As they rustle together saying hello,
Some thin, some smooth, some rough,
There lie the leaves scattered across the floor.

Becky Tolliday (10)
Eastbury Farm JMI & Nursery School, Northwood

The Sea

The sea is as rough as a brick,
As beautiful as a butterfly,
The coral is many different colours,
Colours of the fish,
Colours of the seabed,
Sharks waiting for dinner,
Divers enjoying the scene,
Fish looking for homes,
Dolphins jumping out the water,
Children paddling shallow,
Adults waiting for the sun to go down.

Lauren Slater (9)
Eastbury Farm JMI & Nursery School, Northwood

Squirrels And Birds

Scurrying squirrels
Climbing a tree.
Chirping birds,
Flying over me.
As small as pebbles,
Are squirrels' tiny little paws.
As thin as twigs,
Are birds' small claws.

Kieran Morrison (10)
Eastbury Farm JMI & Nursery School, Northwood

I Am Standing There For You

When I see the water blue,
I am standing there for you.

When I see the leaves rustling
I am standing there for you.

When the autumn leaves fall
I am standing there for you.

When the autumn leaves fall
I see them blow to the trees
The trees see them fall
But I am always standing there for you,
Forever.

Even when bad things happen
I will still be standing there for you.

Stephanie Challis (9)
Eastbury Farm JMI & Nursery School, Northwood

The Early Morning Breeze

Whistling past my ears,
Like a whip lashing past my face.
One second it's here,
And the next minute it's not.

As fast as a hare,
The air having a race.
Or maybe a mystery man blowing out a fire.

Who is that man
And what is his name?
Nobody knows,
Only the wind.

Ellie Weston (10)
Eastbury Farm JMI & Nursery School, Northwood

Trees Are Different In Many Different Ways

Trees are different in many different ways,
Bark, stripy, spotty, white and brown, thick and thin
Old and new.

Twigs fall like canoes in white water
The wind rustles the leaves like the blind shuffling up and down.
Trees leaves, purple red and green
Trees are different in many different ways.

Why are the trees grown in many different places?
Africa, Scotland, Ireland and Wales,
Some trees are great, rich and famous,
Some are useless, poor and unknown,
Trees are tall,
Trees are small,
But trees are different in many different ways.

Kate Miller (11)
Eastbury Farm JMI & Nursery School, Northwood

Little Sister

She wakes in the morning and fills her room with lavender.
Her little voice as soft as the morning breeze.
She goes around the house making no trouble which makes
                                                                           me happy.
Her curly hair is as soft as silk.
She'll sit in front of the TV as still as a statue.
But runs around the garden like a cheetah.
Then she falls to sleep as graceful as a leaf falling from
                                                            a 20ft high tree.

Alexander Butcher (10)
Eastbury Farm JMI & Nursery School, Northwood

Mr Big Tree

That tree, on the corner of the road,
How did it get there?
How did it grow so tall?
Did it start as a twig
And grow and grow and grow?

It started as a shoot and grew 20ft tall!

Are those branches its arms
And that green its hair?

Yes I believe so,
Look it's waving to you,
Go on say hello!

Hello Mr Big Tree, hello, hello, hello!
Do you get very lonely Mr Big Tree?
Shall I bring you back home?

Phebe Brown (11)
Eastbury Farm JMI & Nursery School, Northwood

Water

The rushing water
Of the river,
Rampaging like a charging bull.

With his rushing white hair,
And screaming voice.

Swollen and jumping,
All the way, rough and calm,
Rough and calm.

Adam Gibbor (9)
Eastbury Farm JMI & Nursery School, Northwood

The Oak Tree

The oak tree makes me feel small,
Like an elephant and a mouse.

Its bark is as rough as a front door mat
And its trunk is as thick as concrete.

The gentle rustling of the leaves is soothing and sleepy.

The branches swaying in the breeze
The pigeons nesting in the leaves.

The oak tree is an old, old tree
Don't cut it down, leave it be.

James Nicholas (9)
Eastbury Farm JMI & Nursery School, Northwood

The Hawaiian Beaches

The calm breeze weaving in and out of the palm trees relaxes me.
The air is humid, the fireflies come out like shooting stars
And the moon lights up the night sky.
The distant music, softly playing a traditional Hawaiian song.
The sand as soft as feathers, as white as paper.
The sea as blue as the sky, gently lapping up at the shore.
Looking at the sea, I see a beautiful sunset, the sky painted with
Water-colours pink and orange.
I feel relaxed lying on the soft sand listening to the music
And the sound of gentle waves.

Christine Swain (11)
Eastbury Farm JMI & Nursery School, Northwood

My Mind

My mind works like a never-ending fire,
It just goes on and on
And if I'm concentrating really, really hard,
That's what my mind will focus upon.

It can think of things that others can't think,
That no one can possibly read.
It can picture something small, so menacingly tall,
Though it could be a tiny bead.

It can make things up that no one knows,
Things that just couldn't be real.
Some people say, 'It happens that way,
Because it reflects how you feel.'

Katherine Barraclough (9)
Eastbury Farm JMI & Nursery School, Northwood

The Dancing Sea

The sea heard the fish whispering below.
The sight of the plants dancing below made him glad.
Swaying happily whispering secrets to the sky.

Then dancing happily as the wind comes
Getting confused when people with funny boards come
Then calmly going to sleep
The sea goes to bed.

Rachel Sibson (10)
Eastbury Farm JMI & Nursery School, Northwood

My Hamster Galaxy

My hamster Galaxy is like a fluffy ball
Sleeps in the day and is awake at night
He loves to abseil down the phone wire
He looks like a big bundle of fur all snug and warm.

He has hobbies like doing monkey bars on top of his cage
And squealing like a rabbit
I take him for walks on his red lead.

He thinks he is one of the family, does all the same things
He's like a mouse, he squeaks at the doorbell
He is a member of the family, there every day and will never let
me down.

Chloe Davies (9)
Eastbury Farm JMI & Nursery School, Northwood

My Little Brother

My little brother is a menace but he's really very good.
He likes to be tickled and tries to be like me.
His smile is as big as an elephant.
He is crazy, nice and fun,
But sometimes he's cross, angry, he cries, he hits.
My little brother is a menace, what do you think?

James Price (9)
Eastbury Farm JMI & Nursery School, Northwood

My Brother

He is five years old
He always wears an Arsenal top
And always sticks his hair up.
He likes football, he pretends to be Thierry Henry
Whenever football's on TV he gets his football top
I feel that he's having loads of fun, my brother.

Hayley Graham (9)
Eastbury Farm JMI & Nursery School, Northwood

Mountains

The mountain is like a camel's hump,
It reminds me of a big tree trying to explode into
Millions of pieces of bark.
High above the clouds let it stand.
It feels cold and scary climbing up
And up into the bold, white clouds,
Getting colder and colder,
Darker and darker,
Layers and layers of thick ice,
Tumbling this way and that,
And there is a spillage
Of white paint
Still frozen.

Hannah Stephens (11)
Eastbury Farm JMI & Nursery School, Northwood

Waterfall

Spraying water everywhere, in the air.
Puffing like clouds of smoke coming out of a train.
Water quickly crashing down like boulders falling off a cliff.
A rocky filter free of charge, but very large!
As big as a mountain, as loud as a drum.
Smells like Mother Nature, tastes as fresh as a minty Tic-Tac
Sounds like a rain stick rolling down a hill.

Tessa Clark (10)
Eastbury Farm JMI & Nursery School, Northwood

My Big Brother

My big brother is a big angry monster coming to eat me up.
He's annoying and horrid like your mum when she tells you off.
He hits me and kicks me but that's not all.

He's silly like a clown at school,
He makes the children laugh, but the teacher's mad.
But he goes home all nasty and serious,
I know he's mad at me, argh!

Oh no! his friend is round now, he's going to be extra mean.
'Go away,' he said, 'I hate you.'
So I left.
Now I'm OK he's gone to the sweet shop, I hope he gets
                                                  some for me.

He is a chimpanzee all hairy on his arms
You can hear him snoring, now he's gone to sleep.

He's gone to secondary school, now his uniform is as smart
As my dad when he goes to work.
I wonder if he has got told off yet.

Me and my sister are fighting again
So Lewis comes but hurts me ouch!

He smells like his room - all smelly
But apart from all that he's lovely and I am lucky to have him
But he has to stop saying, 'Cheese!'

Amy Decker (9)
Eastbury Farm JMI & Nursery School, Northwood

The Stars

The stars shot out behind the trees
The stars chased the sun to show it was night
The stars kicked the moon out of the way
The stars bumped into each other and said, 'Ow'
The stars cried because it was morning.

Kitty Corbett (9)
Eastbury Farm JMI & Nursery School, Northwood

Winter Wonders

I watch snowballs fly through the sky,
A bird in flight, panicking, passing a war zone.

A sleigh comes by, a dog pops its head out and says,
'We wish you a Merry Christmas,'
Then moves on into the distance . . .

I see mice scuttling around singing on their back legs,
Looking up for attention but, sometimes, receiving little packages
With treats inside, though many people ignore them and the mice
                                                                  keep singing.

I see ducks learning to skate, I watch a man sell a spinning plate.

I watch frogs wearing ballet shoes, pirouetting,
Twirling on the ice.

Now it is Christmas Eve, I see lights go out,
The voices of cats singing down the street
Wishing everyone a Happy Christmas!

Thirza McDonald (11)
Eastbury Farm JMI & Nursery School, Northwood

Friends

Friends are as helpful as your family would be.
As fun as a party and as important as your mum.
You can spread your secrets anywhere you go.
Friends are water, something you can't live without
Without them your life would turn to shame
'Friends', a word that will bring a smile to your face
So keep your friends forever, you won't regret it.

Sachin Dholakia (10)
Eastbury Farm JMI & Nursery School, Northwood

The Orca

The orca
Strikes with fear
Speaking in the waves.
Touching the top
Of the sun
With its tail
As the tide
Beats the rocks
Crashing the blaze of
Air
Intense of water
Land's far.

Matthew Chong (9)
Eastbury Farm JMI & Nursery School, Northwood

My Little Duck

My friendly duck swims in the jet-black river
My little ducky dives like a submarine
His beak is a powerful thing
His webbed feet help him glide across the water
His feathers next
They help him fly north
Yes that's my little duck.

Jake Thomas (11)
Eastbury Farm JMI & Nursery School, Northwood

Haikus

Did you see the moon
Stealthy as foxes slip down
To the forest clouds?

The moon is up high
The moon is shining brightly
And the sun is too.

Molly Welton (9)
Eastbury Farm JMI & Nursery School, Northwood

Watford FC

Watford FC the joy of most people
The atmosphere was the smell of fresh air weaving in and out
                                                                     of fans.
The sound bounding in your ears like a shockwave.
The smell of the café driving people towards them for a snack.
The kit shining in people's eyes on a late night.
When the ball goes in the silky net, the crowd will pound your ears.
When I watch a Watford match, it reminds me of the goal I scored
                                                                     yesterday.
The team goes in, maybe I'm grumpy, maybe cheerful,
When I go home I go to bed and remember the best time I've had
                                                                at a Watford match.

Reece Thomas (9)
Eastbury Farm JMI & Nursery School, Northwood

Roller Coaster

Sit in my seat, get ready to go,
Terrified and happy, I'm both of them.

As fast as a rocket and as slow as a snail
Sometimes I see people waving at me,
Moving dots in the distance.

Speeding along, banging my head, my arms are numb
And my legs are dead.
The wind in my face, like a cold winter blizzard
A racing car at top speed.

We start to slow down,
I've had so much fun
It was like Concorde at full power.

David Braham (10)
Eastbury Farm JMI & Nursery School, Northwood

Volcanic Volcanoes

The fire crackling on the great mounds of baking sulphur,
The sulphur as hot as a burning sun with huge flames drowning
                                                                  the cold,
Human beings melting from the sauna into dust
The smell as revolting as 1,000,000 rotten eggs on a bad day
So much steam it is a blinding fog,
The touch of the ground is as dry as a bone
People in the crater laughing from the heat.
                Volcanic volcanoes
                Sizzling red-hot.

Harry Lock (10)
Eastbury Farm JMI & Nursery School, Northwood

The Swan

The swan, beak so strong with its long slender neck
Eating as it goes like my brother Harry
It's swimming as fast as Michael Thorpe in the Olympics.

Then looking underwater, for its nice fishy prey, now coming
Up from the deep blue.

Now going to a boat for its lovely bread
And another and another and so it goes and goes.
Then it's time for bed as it waddles up to its nice cosy bed. *Shhh!*

Charlie Millard (9)
Eastbury Farm JMI & Nursery School, Northwood

Haiku

The moon is silver
At night the moon shines brightly
Going out at dusk.

James Hayes (9)
Eastbury Farm JMI & Nursery School, Northwood

The London Double Header

Players run, kick, pass and tackle, a wrestling match in disguise.
The kicker steps up, places the ball on the tee,
Kicks it so sweetly, like a bird in flight through the posts,
Three points.
The fans cheer and down their Guinness, they are having fun,
Like children in a playground.
This is not just any rugby match, it is a jewel of a rugby match!
The smell of hot dogs, burgers and chips all fill my nose in one
                                                                                 pleasant surprise!
The atmosphere is overwhelming 'Swing low' ringing around
                                                                                                        the ground.
Go Sarries! As they mount a raid.
Sarries score, Ben Skirving it is! Come on Glen Jackson,
Convert the try, a clumsy kick, it wobbles and dives, does it go over?
No it's a miss! Better luck next time.
Saracens lose, but do not despair
For we've won a prize from the Guinness guys there.
What a day, I hope we go again, it's like opening a present.
You never know what's inside.

Harry Millard (10)
Eastbury Farm JMI & Nursery School, Northwood

The Eagle

The eagle glides as fast as a cheetah,
And squawks as loud as a pack of lions.
They intimidate us with their immense beaks and bulging eyes.

The eagle circles its prey like a group of hyenas,
And attack their food in a blink of an eye,
Eagles are planes roaring through the sky.

Stuart Patrick (10)
Eastbury Farm JMI & Nursery School, Northwood

My Dog

He's cuddly and soft
My teddy dog is
Fuzzy and loving
Warm like a grill
His tail is a spring, jumping around
Woofing and barking
That terrible sound
His teeth are like daggers opening wide
Quick he might bite
You but phew,
He's not a hound
When the bell rings
He gets all excited
Grabbing his bone
Ready to party
He's always there
Like a flowing river,
Never running out
Just sitting still as a feather
Then lying down like a
Smooth pebble, sleeping peacefully.

Franceska Gudiens (10)
Eastbury Farm JMI & Nursery School, Northwood

Spiders

Our eight legged friends
Drive my dad round the bend
They're blood-sucking vampires
Wrapping up flies in silk
Spiders don't bite
Unless they have a fright
They're crawly and speedy
Sometimes quite greedy like a big fat toad
They don't like the light like a fish in a trench.

Ryan Kirkman (9)
Eastbury Farm JMI & Nursery School, Northwood

Julie

Julie is really fun to play with
She tells really funny jokes
She is my sister as well.
Sometimes she is as bossy as a teacher.

She can be as quiet as a feather falling down into the river
And as noisy as an elephant stamping
And making a noise with its trunk.

She has blue eyes and she looks nice.

Julie's a clown,
She makes you laugh your head off.

Sometimes she and Shannon hide away from me
But then me and Julie hide away from Shannon.

She is a bit fussy,
She acts like a queen because she is the oldest.

Julie is really nice and funny
She is really kind.

Sarah Mattson (11)
Eastbury Farm JMI & Nursery School, Northwood

The Stars

The stars shine with all their might
There are millions and millions in sight
They shine in the dark sky at night
The stars are really bright.

They dance around the sky
They look as small as breadcrumbs
They shine with their beady eyes
They wave their dangly legs.

The stars look so silvery
They are as precious as jewellery.

Ali-Reza Daya (10)
Eastbury Farm JMI & Nursery School, Northwood

The Utterly Unnecessary

Make me talk
I won't speak
I won't move my lips
Or open my beak.

>I didn't do it
>I didn't do it
>Don't tell me I did
>Cos I didn't.

Would I want to put slime
On the teacher's desk?
Would I want to put
Glue on her chair?

>And still you think
>That I'd do such a
>Thing as put green
>Paint in her hair.

She told me I cheated in maths
But I only do that in a race
So she told me off and I
Told her off too
By throwing a pie in her face.

Abbie Neale
Eastbury Farm JMI & Nursery School, Northwood

Solar System

The Earth is home to you and me,
It floats in the solar system so gleefully.
There are ten planets circling the sun,
That doesn't sound much fun.

There are many, many moons,
Each has a sand dune.
It is not very hard to see,
How wonderful the solar system can be.

Brennan Cleveland (10)
Eastbury Farm JMI & Nursery School, Northwood

My Weird Brother

My little brother is weird,
He leaps around like a trampoliner
He runs around like a rugby player
He knocks everything over,
But never hurts himself.

He takes his favourite bear with him wherever he goes,
He plays with it wherever he knows,
He takes it with him, wherever he knows.

He likes to pick up snails and spiders
And he really likes to pick bits up,
From the floor - he is a human hoover.

He likes to taste new things,
But his favourite thing to eat is
     Bananas

He is a monkey,
He has one every day.

Katie Allday (9)
Eastbury Farm JMI & Nursery School, Northwood

Kittens Like Mittens

Six little kittens
As warm as mittens
Lapping up the milk
Their fur as soft as silk
All in bed those sleepy heads
It's time to say goodnight.

When morning comes
Let's have some fun
Playing all day long
Hey! What was that bong?
Oh it's dinner
If we don't eat we'll get thinner and thinner
Mmm . . . salmon and chicken delight.

Karis Parfitt (10)
Eastbury Farm JMI & Nursery School, Northwood

The Sun

The sun is a yellow football on fire, screaming, 'Help!'
Always waving in the mornings and always going for a stroll
                                                    down the road.
The sun is telling me to kick it in the back of the net
The moon said to the sun he is his best friend
The sun loves to dance with my mum
He loves to have competitions with James on the violin
But James always wins!
The sun always likes to write
He likes going to school
He has neat writing
And at the end of the day
We just sit down and watch telly and have a nice cold drink.

Steff Capittelli (10)
Eastbury Farm JMI & Nursery School, Northwood

The Rainforest

I hear the noise of the wild leaves falling,
The slither of unusual snakes,
I walk upon the footprints of the roaring lions,
Leading towards the crocodiles' lakes.

Toucans swooping down on me,
Upon the treetops of the highest trees,
I look around, a bunny in front of me,
Amongst the sound of the buzzing bees.

I see the different creatures around me
It must be a different world.
To be allowed in a deep rainforest.
And even the smallest animals tucked up warm and curled.

Lucy Miah (9)
Eastbury Farm JMI & Nursery School, Northwood

Beautiful Charms

Falling and twirling round and round
Down and down.
It's as fast as a whirlwind spinning around.
The snowflakes look like spiderwebs
Dancing softly in the air.
Looking so bare.
They race against the snow to the ground,
Not making a single sound.
So blue, so white,
Flying and crying like a kite.
Small and tiny you can hardly see them
Gliding swiftly as clear as a gem
You want to hold them in your palm,
Yet they're so delicate like a charm.
So don't pick them up or they will break
Just look at them, the beautiful snowflakes.

Georgia Barton (10)
Eastbury Farm JMI & Nursery School, Northwood

Hurricane Troubles

Lightning and rain
Blood and pain

        Floods and deaths
        Kills the pests

Thunder and fire
Hit the spire

        Tornadoes and wind
        Makes people spin

    Because of all
    The hurricane troubles.

Kourosh Khodabakhsh (9)
Eastbury Farm JMI & Nursery School, Northwood

In A Desolate World

Here I am
I'm all alone
Where is everybody?
Why aren't you here?
A secret tear of mine escapes.
A tiny drop of water on a sawdust-covered ground.
You may not think much of me
For I am not human.
One thing that does not matter,
In the desolate world of today.
Back hundreds and hundreds of years,
I was admired by all my friends
The tallest of us all.
Who could see over the green.
Helpful I was to people as well.
But now you have betrayed me.
Please, I ask you to stop.

Charlotte McDonagh (10)
Eastbury Farm JMI & Nursery School, Northwood

Jungle

Monkeys cheeky just like me
They all say, 'Hee hee hee.'
Slithering snakes coming through
Unhappy like a dangerous crew
Parrot, parrot on a branch
I don't have a chance
Lion's scary, but not to me
All they want is to be free
Night and day
All the animals play.

Sophie Williams (10)
Eastbury Farm JMI & Nursery School, Northwood

Oh What Do I See?

Looking down there I see
Lots of creatures running free,
Then I see flowers looking at the sky
So I decide to ask them why?
'Oh flowers, why do you stare
Looking freely through the air?'
'Oh sun we do not look at the skies
We look at you where beauty lies.'
There I see butterflies sway,
Round and round the insects play.
What's this, I see the clouds mumble,
Crying and moaning full of grumble.
All I hear is the trees whispering,
Through the air it sounds like whistling.
Squirrels run, rabbits walk
Then listen to the flowers talk.
Grass dances, moves to the beat,
Hot and bothered by my heat.

Mia Zambakides (10)
Eastbury Farm JMI & Nursery School, Northwood

Autumn

A ll of a sudden the air is getting cool
   And many leaves are starting to fall
U nder the leaves the hedgehogs start to go
   To make their beds in preparation for next season's snow
T rees are changing colour every day
   Red to orange to yellow until all the leaves have blown away
U p and down the squirrels run
   Busy collecting food for when there is none
M igrating birds fill up the bright sky
   If they stayed for the cold winter they might die
N ights start to fall early as the clocks go back an hour
   People retreat to their houses as winter seems to be
                          gaining power.

Evie Gardiner (9)
Eastbury Farm JMI & Nursery School, Northwood

Volcano Burns

Hot as a fire-breathing dragon
It erupts like a tiger ready to pounce
Like a computer ready to be turned on
It hunts all day and night for its chance to erupt

Caution it might be dangerous
It could burn off a hand if you touch it
Like an elephant stampeding through the jungle
Listen you might be able to hear it.

Bubbly and hot all over its body
It might come alive and gobble you up
Like someone eating all their food down
Now it is calming down and going back to sleep

Now it is asleep, quiet and peaceful
Calm and lazy it sleeps on and on
Like a bird flying beautifully across the sky
It is slowly turning back to rock.

Lauren Smith (10)
Eastbury Farm JMI & Nursery School, Northwood

Bunnies

Bunnies are grey
And they never frown
I love them so
Their little grey tails wagging
Hopping through a ring
Always very happy
Jumping with joy.

Katherine Head (10)
Eastbury Farm JMI & Nursery School, Northwood

Snow

Snow is cold
I like to hold
The snow which is white
And I can even bite
The cold wet snow
Which falls from the sky
In my mouth it comes

My favourite thing abut snow
Is that I can build snowmen
With a lovely cotton scarf
Which makes me laugh and laugh

I like to throw a snowball
And when the snow starts to fall
I throw snowballs in people's faces
Although they get stuck in their braces.

Charlotte Bignall (10)
Eastbury Farm JMI & Nursery School, Northwood

Autumn Days

Autumn leaves change from crisp golden to red,
Almost time for the bears to go to bed,
'Buzz, buzz' buzzing the bees buzz no more,
Without autumn it's such a bore.

Autumn's flowers are beginning to die
All the trees are getting dry,
Almost time for Jack Frost to come out and play
All in a day's work for an autumn day.

Lauren Hatton (10)
Eastbury Farm JMI & Nursery School, Northwood

My Genesis Poem

God made the Earth in six days,
Each day he said a different say.
Day one he said, 'Let there be light,'
And it came to the Earth and made a different sight.
Day two he said, 'Separate the water,
Make it so it's a little shorter.'
Day three he said, 'Let there be land,
And so it will be covered in sand.'
Day four he said, 'Let there be night,
Make sure it's not at all bright.'
Day five he said, 'Let there be fish,
Make them become our favourite dish.'
Day six he said, 'Let there be people,
Make them go to the precious steeple.'
That is the end of the creation story.

Sameera Hamid (11)
Eastbury Farm JMI & Nursery School, Northwood

Monsters

Monster creeps around,
Scaring everyone he has found.
He only comes out at night
He's allergic to the light.

He doesn't have a brain
He can only cause pain,
He is very hairy,
He is Mr Scary.
When you are in bed,
He comes out of the shed
With no head
Instead
He is blood-red.

Sam Southwell (10)
Eastbury Farm JMI & Nursery School, Northwood

The Antarctica

Two large daggers come out of their mouth
It's a big brown lump,
It's got beady eyes,
Brown as brown can get,
Like a seal,
Long, long whiskers with a pointed tip,
Their flippers go hyper and flip,
This is the beast of Antarctica.

As cuddly as a big stuffed toy,
As white as a sheet of paper,
Its warm fluffy coat,
Its pink button nose,
Its pink teddy ears,
Its big paws,
But beware, it's as dangerous as a shark,
Its home is Antarctica.

Their feet like flippers,
They waddle side to side,
Their colour black and white,
Their wings help them swim,
Slippery skin,
An Olympic swimmer.

Charlotte Melinek (10)
Eastbury Farm JMI & Nursery School, Northwood

Happy Vegetables

H appy vegetables growing in the soil
A pples are nice and juicy
R ipe tomatoes growing in the ground
V egetables are nice and juicy
E ating the vegetables is so good
S itting in the garden watching them grow
T omatoes shoot out of the ground.

Samuel Castle (7)
Garlinge Junior School, Margate

Autumn, Bright Autumn

I can see glittering puddles,
Bouncy conkers,
Bright, light yellow leaves,
Green grass shining on the moonlight,
Puddles bright on a summer night.

I can hear dripping from the dusty old drain,
Loud thunder makes the pain,
Children running on the crunchy rustling leaves.

I can feel the cold breeze chattering my teeth
Cold rain dripping on my face
My soft teddy snuggled up warm.

Abbey Golder (8)
Garlinge Junior School, Margate

Euro Disney

Oh Euro Disney, you're the best place
That the builders could ever make.
You are a fun place in France far away
But the disappointing thing is you have to pay!

Oh Legoland is the most fun place
But got no time to waste
I've got rides to go on, shows to see
It's all about me.

Oh Dreamland you've got rides waiting for me
I'm always working, I need to be free.

Charley Jackson-Powell (7)
Garlinge Junior School, Margate

An Autumn Night

All different coloured leaves,
People walking past in warm sleeves,
Shining conkers on the ground,
When I walk over them I stumble to the ground,
Stars in the sky,
Twinkling up high,
Rushing, gushing wind,
Swirling around me,
A dog is barking in the dark
As the moon shines down on me,
Tweeting birds in the trees,
With their fluffy feathers in the breeze,
Flowers closing, flowers sleeping,
And that's the end of an autumn evening.

Rebecca Mann (8)
Garlinge Junior School, Margate

My Autumn Poem

See, see, I see lots of things,
Things like leaves and conkers.
Autumn, autumn is here today
Children playing every day
Mornings, mornings, cold and damp
Hot drinks in the day keeping us warm
Warm, warm it is so good to be warm
Hot, hot, it is not hot
Feel, feel, I feel lots of things
I feel like a cold snow girl
I like the feel of leaves and conkers
I hear, hear, I hear lots of things,
I hear birds and the children
Children all over the place.

Holly Hill (8)
Garlinge Junior School, Margate

The Autumn Leaves

The acorns and conkers are falling off the tree
Is it nearly autumn, I just wonder what autumn is?
Leaves are changing colour every single day
The colours are red, gold, brown and orange
Birds are squeaking for sticks for nests.

I can feel the wind blow across my face
There are squirrels running up and down the tree.
They are collecting nuts for winter,
The wind is blowing the leaves away,
To a far, far away country, a cold one too.

The leaves are curling and falling apart
Everybody stamped on them
I just don't know why.

Jemma Eccott (8)
Garlinge Junior School, Margate

Autumn Feelings

I can see the golden coloured leaves falling and crunching,
As people stand on them
And the black and white clouds letting the water fall
I can hear the leaves rustling in the trees
And the birds tweeting and hanging in the trees
And the wind howling at me
I can feel the cold breeze blowing at me
And trying to push me out of the way
And the raindrops falling on me.

Dexter Hamilton (8)
Garlinge Junior School, Margate

Autumn

Sudden squalls of chilly rain
As the seasons move around again

Hustling hedgehogs, hibernating happily

The leaves are falling
The leaves are crunching
The leaves are hard and punching
The leaves are brown, yellow and red.

The trees are colourful
The trees are hard
The trees have sparks
The trees are rustling.

Suddenly the wind gets up
Suddenly the wind is strong,
Suddenly the wind is high
Suddenly the wind is calm.

The birds are singing in the trees
With the spiky conkers falling.

Louise Cannon (8)
Garlinge Junior School, Margate

The Sea

It's as cold as ice
It's choppy and rough
The sea sparkles on a sunny day
The birds fly high above in the sky
Whilst the fish swim deep down below
Boats float along the surface
Churning up waves.

Ben Sheppard (7)
Garlinge Junior School, Margate

Winter, Spring, Summer And Autumn

Winter, spring, summer and autumn
Winter, spring, summer and cold.
Winter, spring, summer and autumn
Winter, spring and summer is all.

You can see all the leaves changing
You can see squirrels getting nuts
You can see the trees rustling
And you can see all the squirrels munch.

Winter, spring, summer and autumn
Winter, spring, summer and cold.
Winter, spring, summer and autumn
Winter, spring and summer is all.

And now autumn is nearly over,
And all the leaves start changing colour,
And then it all starts getting colder,
And then it gets colder and warmer.

Winter, spring, summer and autumn
Winter, spring, summer and cold.
Winter, spring, summer and autumn
Winter, spring and summer is all!

Courtney Clarke (8)
Garlinge Junior School, Margate

Dancing

I danced in the street
I danced on the stars
I danced all around the world
And then into France.

I danced in the corridors,
I danced in the class,
I danced in the hall,
And danced more and more.

Jessica Voss (7)
Garlinge Junior School, Margate

Autumn

I can see the dark mysterious shadows hiding mischievously
The grass lying silently in the sunlight
I can see the red, brown and yellow leaves on the bold trees
The golden sun is shining brightly.

I can hear the leaves crunching as I step on them
The sound of footsteps surround my ears.
I can hear the birds singing peacefully
The voices of children passing by.

I can feel the strong spirit of the wind brushing against my face
The sunrays beating down on me from the bright blue sky
I can feel goosebumps when the breeze gets hold of my
Arms and legs,
Deep down I feel some calmness and peace.

Laura Robertshaw (8)
Garlinge Junior School, Margate

In Autumn

I can see . . .
Conkers falling to the ground
Leaves falling from the trees
Kids jumping into leaves.

I can feel . . .
The colours of the leaves
And the wind blowing softly and nice

I can hear . . .
Children jumping into leaves
And hedgehogs rustling in the bushes
And birds singing all day long.

Kieran Doyle (8)
Garlinge Junior School, Margate

Chocolate

Smooth yummy chocolate melting in the sun
Look quick it's turning into yum.
People eating chocolate everywhere
Look quick it's over there.
I want chocolate not sweets
Give me something good to eat.
If you don't I'm sure I'll die
And chocolate too, I'm only joking that's just a lie.
There's all sorts of chocolate, nutty, plain, dark and fruit
But best of all there's the Twix.
I love my chocolate all to bits,
If anything happened
I would go and put it back in fashion.
I would love to make a chocolate river,
Like Willy Wonka and be very famous.
If I ever invented a new chocolate bar
I would have one every day
And call it chocolate.
It would love being the greatest chocolate bar invented
It would be so great just to have a chocolate bar each and every day.
If I never had a chocolate bar in my life,
I would cry my eyes out and never go to bed
That would be bad and I'm glad that isn't me.

Aidan Hepworth (7)
Garlinge Junior School, Margate

Autumn

Autumn is here once again
The animals want to make their den
Ready for hibernation
This is a big occasion
No more sun
The growing has been done.

Harriet Chapman (8)
Garlinge Junior School, Margate

Autumn

I can see crumpled leaves on the dirty floor
The birds flying in the sky.
I can see the bushes as green as a pear
Autumn leaves swirling to the ground.

I can hear the rain swiftly hit the ground
Autumn leaves gently fall off the thick branch.
I can hear the rain as it drips down the window
Birds singing sweetly in the breeze.

I can feel the wind as it rubs against my skin
Goosebumps appearing on my arms.
I can feel the shining sun gleaming on my face
Autumn leaves flying everywhere.

Lauren Hart (8)
Garlinge Junior School, Margate

The Beach

Beach, beach, come to the beach
Come and have a ice cream on the beach.

Beach, beach, it's really fun,
Come and have a paddle in the sea.

Beach, beach, come to the beach,
Build a sandcastle on the beach.

Beach, beach, it's getting late
Let's go home from the beach.

Charne Welch (8)
Garlinge Junior School, Margate

Autumn Is Here

Autumn is here
Give a cheer
Leaves are falling
Give a calling.

Animals hibernate
You see if you can state
Collect conkers
Or you'll be bonkers.

Stay in
Eat your din'
Keep warm
Don't bother about the lawn.

Don't be mean
Support your home team
Be a dear
Harvest is here
Back to school
Assembly in the hall
Winter's here
At the end of the year.

Simon Boyd (8)
Garlinge Junior School, Margate

Leaves Are Floating

Leaves are floating to the ground
Yellow, orange, red and brown.
The trees have no leaves they're dead and bare
It looks like a skeleton from way over there.
Other trees are not dead and bare
But in a few weeks the leaves won't be there.
Look at the leaves while they still last,
They've been beautiful in their past.
The leaves will come back in another year
So don't despair some are still here.

Amy Mallett (10)
Garlinge Junior School, Margate

Autumn

Sudden squalls of chilly rain
As the seasons move around again.
All the leaves turning orange, yellow and brown,
They start to die and fall to the ground.
The squirrels start to collect some nuts,
And put it in their tree trunk.

I can feel the prickly conker shells,
I can feel the breeze cooling me down,
I feel the leaves falling off trees and landing on me,
I feel the drops of chilly rain.

I hear the leaves brushing on the ground,
I can hear the children running around,
I hear the trees swaying side to side,
I hear the sound of wind blowing stuff in my eyes.

Erustus Agutu (8)
Garlinge Junior School, Margate

France

Flying in the air
Flying everywhere
Looking down to a town
And looking in the air
Landing down to France
It was really hot
And I loved it a lot
Going to the beach
Landing in the sea
I had great fun
Fishing in the sea
I'd love to go
To have a ice cream
Yes please!

Aimee Chamberlain (7)
Garlinge Junior School, Margate

Harvest

Farmers collecting all the crops,
Making beer from the hops.
Leaves are falling to the ground,
While conkers are being found,
Foals are jumping all around,
While bears are hibernating underground.

Birds are flying to Spain,
So they can miss all the rain,
Flowers are starting to get old,
And all the crops are being sold,
People are having a feast,
With lots of food and yeast.

Wheat is turning into bread,
All the poor are being fed.
It's starting to get cold,
And things are starting to grow mould,
Soon it's going to snow,
And animals are starting to go.

India Toomey (9)
Garlinge Junior School, Margate

Autumn

I can see the crumpled leaves scattered across the ground
The birds flying through the howling wind.
I can see the patchy grass turning brown,
Autumn trees looking bold also standing proudly.

I can hear the rain dripping heavily splashing into puddles
The birds singing calmly through the rough sky.
Autumn branches snapping furiously off the trees,
The leaves rustling angrily trying to get away.

I can feel the breeze blowing gently on my face
When I pick a crumbled leaf up I feel it crunching up.
I can feel the bumpy bark against the bold tree,
The grass going hard as I spread my hand across it.

Chloe Roberts (8)
Garlinge Junior School, Margate

Harvest Time

It's harvest time,
It's harvest time,
My favourite time of year,
Lots of lovely sounds visit my ear.

You can hear some birds,
Singing 1, 2, 3,
Oh look some conkers,
One for you and me.

There are some field mice,
Hibernating of course,
Look over there,
It is a horse.

Oh look there are some trees,
They look like men with knobbly knees,
With crispy leaves brown and gold,
I reckon it is very old.

Be grateful to harvest,
It comes every year,
Winter is coming very near.

Elizabeth Randall (9)
Garlinge Junior School, Margate

Vampire Sim

There once was a vampire called Sim
I don't think he'd got any limb,
I went to his castle at night
I had a terrible fright
I ran outside as fast as I can
And got in a big pink van.

I got away
Pretty fine, pretty OK
I must say
It was a terrible day.

Tom Webb (10)
Gladstone Primary School, Barry

There Once Was A Girl Called Jill

There once was a girl called Jill,
Who fancied a man called Bill
She did something one day
Which scared him away
And that was the end of Bill!

I know someone you know,
Who turned herself into a crow
She flew away
And was found that day,
Stuck in a pile of snow!

There once was a man called Lee
Who got lost out at sea
He called for his friend,
'Cause they've been friends till the end
But no one knows where he could be!

Hannah James (10)
Gladstone Primary School, Barry

My Dream

In my dream I'd like to be an astronaut and fly to the sky,
But why does it happen just in my dream?
Oh why, oh why, oh why?
In my dream I'd like to be a famous movie star
That could just be round the corner or it could be far.
In my dream everything comes alive,
Everything up to the tiniest beehive.
In my dream I could be a janitor to an acrobat,
I could be anything my heart desires even a top hat.

Sophie Owens (11)
Gladstone Primary School, Barry

My Family And Friends

My family always care for me
My mum feeds me hot meals all the time
My dad is the same, he is very kind
And my brothers, they're fine
My dog is very playful and lays on my lap
My friends at school come up to me when I am sad
My cousins are very friendly they always make me smile
My aunties are great to me they buy me lots of stuff
And my uncles are OK they give me lots of money
Every time I smile they always find it funny
And I hope you liked my poem about my friends and family.

Amy James (10)
Gladstone Primary School, Barry

The School

The school is fun,
I laugh and shout
I have fun and the teachers are very nice
I go to catch up every Monday and Tuesday
We have got a big field and playground, two of them
And I have loads of friends and I am good all the time.

Ritchie Aspinall
Gladstone Primary School, Barry

Rain

I watch the rain falling down on my glass window
Making a pattern on my window.
The rain falls off my wall
Then into the drain
Each pitter-patter on my glass, it goes back in my drain.

James Cassam (10)
Gladstone Primary School, Barry

The Jungle

I once walked in the jungle
I heard this weird sound,
I saw a big gorilla
Dancing on the ground.

I could not believe my eyes
When I saw this lovely creature,
A tiger should I say
Eating a dirty, smelly teacher.

I came upon a river
And I saw a pink flamingo,
A pelican reading a paper?
Of course they're playing bingo!

It's nearly the end of my journey
It's time for me to go,
I will miss what I've seen today
There's just one thing you must know,
Standing by my helicopter,
Is an elephant dressed like a man,
He is ready to go too
In a mini pink van!

Carrianne Rogers (10)
Gladstone Primary School, Barry

The Moon

As I looked out to the dark sky
The moon was high
The moon was half-dark, half-light
It was very bright.

Connor Rowlands
Gladstone Primary School, Barry

Barney McFee

I know a man called Barney McFee
Who fell down the stairs and broke his knee.
He went to the hospital in a rush,
He tipped off his wheelchair which made him blush.

His girlfriend Ms Scooby,
Bought him a ruby
Aunty Mrs Powers,
Bought him some flowers.

On Friday he was free,
With his mended old knee
So he scurried to his house,
Like a furry little mouse.

Jacques Sloman (10)
Gladstone Primary School, Barry

Lucky

My dog's name is Lucky
She is a joker and always likes a fuss
Whenever she is nutty, she's always so funny,
She looks like chocolate and has black splodges.
She loves her dinner and loves her walks,
Her favourite hobbies are eating and sleeping.
She is so much fun.

Ellie Goldsby
Gladstone Primary School, Barry

Dave The Alien

There once was an alien called Dave,
He had a chewing gum he wanted to save,
So he put it in his pocket,
He forgot to lock it,
I guess it was one of those days.

Ryan Jones (10)
Gladstone Primary School, Barry

My Birthday In May

It's the 29th of May
It's my birthday.

It's chocolate cake,
Which I'll make,
Then I'll bake.

It's the 29th of May,
It's my birthday.

It's balloons,
Like the moon,
It says it's nearly June.

It's the 29th of May,
It's my birthday.

Everyone says . . .
. . . hip hip hooray!

Jannat Ahmed (10)
Gladstone Primary School, Barry

Animals

A is for antelope which runs very cool
N is for newt which swims in the pool
I is for iguana which walks very slow
M is for mammal, swims with a glow
A is for ape which swings from branch to branch
L is for lion which does a beautiful dance
S is for seal that claps and claps
    And those are the animals that can do a tap.

Lucy Dimond (10)
Gladstone Primary School, Barry

Barry Island

Barry Island's the most beautiful place I have ever seen,
I think I will go there all the time when I am a teen.
With its golden sands and brownish sea,
All of this appeals to me.

And of course number 7, my favourite place to go,
It never rains on my parade when I'm coming I'm sure they know.
The family meets and friends galore,
We have fun, games, laughter and much more.

There's Mandy's Diner and Mr Chips,
I love the taste when they touch my lips.
There's Hyper Value and Fortes Café,
In there they serve coffee and latté.

Of course Marine Drive is a very important place also,
My grampa's ashes are there and that's the place I love to go.
Last but not least Jackson Bay,
Where you just might find me roaming today!

Georgia Graham (10)
Gladstone Primary School, Barry

The Nice Teacher At School

I like the teacher at my school
Because she lets
Us go in the pool
She lets us comb
And plait her hair
She gives us sweets
And loads of treats

And every day
She comes to school
She makes it very, very cool
Now we are in Year 6
We can do more tricks.

Rhia Dutton (10)
Gladstone Primary School, Barry

Important Things!

Music, music different kinds,
Hear the music in your minds.
Like the music, feel the beat,
Sing in the house and dance in the street.

I have a lot of very close friends,
Like Georgia, Rosie, Lucy, it depends.
Whether or not we'll break friends,
But we'll still be together till the end.

And now I go onto my family,
Mum, Dad, brother and everybody.
My family is a very important thing to me,
And when I move out, I'll be adventurous and free!

Chaliese Anderson-Ludvigsen (10)
Gladstone Primary School, Barry

Storm

Thunderous crashes, lightning flashes,
Cars flying, children crying
Trees flying through the air
Houses falling with despair
Tornado destroying anything in its path
Watch out of its fearful wrath.

Franklin Roe (11)
Gladstone Primary School, Barry

Oh Why?

I stand above scalding lava,
Wishing to see a sad drama,
I am really scared,
I would prefer to have a nightmare,
I walk across that wobbly bridge,
I feel as cold as a fridge,
I shiver,
I quiver,
I crumble,
I rumble,
The feel of getting burnt,
I really have learnt,
Huffing,
Puffing,
Chattering,
Clattering,
Oh why did I walk across that bridge?

Chantelle Selby
Gladstone Primary School, Barry

Lightning

Pitter-patter, strike, slam, bang.
Lightning killing and streaking across the world.
Knowing that it keeps its secrets from me.
Tick-tock, time running slowly
Waiting to strike my city.
I am shivering out of my wits
I see a tree being struck and the tiles falling off the roof.
It is so scary to be home alone in a lightning storm.
I am eating my meal, help me someone.

Jessica Lant
Gladstone Primary School, Barry

My Best Friend

My bestest friend is Carrie, she loves dogs
She loves to sing to pop.
I have known Carrie for seven years
I even share my tears with her
She makes me laugh
And she knitted me a scarf
That's what I think of Carrie.

My bestest friend is Carrie
We sometimes go down the beach
And even share sweets
And nothing will stop us from staying together forever
Or will it?

Jade Rees
Gladstone Primary School, Barry

The Frosty Mountain!

When I walk up the cold frosty mountain,
I see people drinking out the cold icy fountain.
You've got to be careful you don't slip down,
The look of your parents is such a frown.

The cold snowy breeze makes you shiver inside,
The width of the mountain is very wide.
You get inside by the warm summery fire,
It is such a huge desire.

Kelly Alford (10)
Gladstone Primary School, Barry

The Lord Of The Galaxy

When it was made, what was there?
Not even a star to watch and stare.
These words we speak today and now
Were not even established but how?
Not even a colour, a word, a thing
Not a man, a woman, was there a king?
Did he make it all but how was he made?
Was it a woman, Venus, Sedna or Jade?
But how was there nothing, what was it?
A colour, a shade, a planet, how did it fit?
But no one knows what was there
A man, a woman, a thing to care.

Elliott Clissold (11)
Gladstone Primary School, Barry

The Witches

The witches creep dead in night,
When there's never any light,
Dressed all in black,
With a broom across their back,
When the sun appears,
The witches disappear,
Without a trace,
Never to show their face,
They run far and wide,
To forever hide.
They run to somewhere dark
Where they hear no dog bark.

Elise Tyler
Gladstone Primary School, Barry

My Bestest Friend, Jade

My bestest friend is Jade,
I've known for seven years,
We like to sing and dance together,
And even share our tears,
And nothing, and I really mean nothing, will stop us from
Staying together forever.

My bestest friend is Jade,
I've known for seven years,
We sometimes go down the beach together and play with our
Buckets and spades,
And we go in the arcades and win lots of things for each other,
And nothing, and I really mean nothing, will stop us from
Staying together forever.

Carrie Aspinall
Gladstone Primary School, Barry

Tigers

Every pounce and every kill,
As he stays in the grass very still.
His teeth so powerful and sharp like knives
And they match his glowing eyes.
He fights for his pride
As he says, 'Step aside.'
His face is cute and furry,
And his whiskers all curly.
His senses are so strong,
He never gets anything wrong.

Charlotte Mills
Gladstone Primary School, Barry

Scary Night

I hear scratches on my door,
And I get goose bumps like never before.
Then my lights flicker on and off,
Then I see a flying kitchen cloth.
All of a sudden all goes black,
And a voice comes from the back.
It says, 'Open the door,' so I go and
'Argh!'

Sam Williams (10)
Gladstone Primary School, Barry

Football Mad

I walk into a match for my first time holding my dad's hands,
I sit down as the crowd goes wild,
No one can hear my cheer
Then my ears pop as a man shouts in my ear
But I love the way my heart flows for football
And they kick the ball on the volley.

Sam Hillier (10)
Gladstone Primary School, Barry

The Farmer

The farmer's name was Bob,
He grew corn on the cob,
Then aliens came
And took him to Spain
And so he lost his job.

Nathan Richards (11)
Gladstone Primary School, Barry

Dog Show

Dog show today,
Oh dear, oh dear,
Dog show today.
That's when I saw,
I saw it, the dog,

Walking up and down.
Round and round,
And then stood,
And then walked again.
With its hair swaying,
Swaying in the breeze,
It won first place.
I was scared,
Should I congratulate this dog or not?
I did.
The lady kind as ever,
She let me touch its fur so soft,
So soft I couldn't stop.
She went away with her dog,
And disappeared into the fog.

Ffion McCullough (10)
Gladstone Primary School, Barry

The Dancer

Watch the dancer whirl and twirl
When she wears her silver pearls.
As she dances her hair will curl,
Round and round oh what a girl.

Spinning, twisting, floating high,
Waves of satin streaming by.
Her shoes move so fast,
She can almost fly.
But why does she dance
And make people cry?

Sophie McCabe
Gladstone Primary School, Barry

Ten Happy Schoolboys
(Based on 'Ten Little Schoolboys' by A A Milne)

Ten happy schoolboys standing in a line;
One fell down
And then there were nine.

Nine happy schoolboys stayed up late;
One didn't get up,
And then there were eight.

Eight happy schoolboys going up to Heaven;
One met God,
And then there were seven.

Seven happy schoolboys carrying sticks;
One hit his head
And then there were six.

Six happy schoolboys near a hive;
One got chased,
And then there were five.

Five happy schoolboys knocking on doors;
One wifey came out,
And then there were four.

Four happy schoolboys up a tree:
One didn't get down,
And then there were three.

Three happy schoolboys went for a poo;
One didn't come back
And then there were two.

Two happy schoolboys shot a gun;
One bullet backfired
And then there was one.

One sad schoolboy had no fun;
He walked slowly home,
And then there were none.

Rhian Gall (11)
Hayshead Primary School, Arbroath

Ten Happy Schoolboys
(Based on 'Ten Little Schoolboys' by A A Milne)

Ten happy schoolboys went out to climb;
One ran out of time,
And then there were nine.

Nine happy schoolboys were out late;
One got grounded,
And then there were eight.

Eight happy schoolboys went to Heaven;
One went to Hell,
Now there were seven.

Seven happy schoolboys playing tricks;
One got caught,
Then there were six.

Six happy schoolboys at a hive;
One got stung,
Then there were five.

Five happy schoolboys were at the shore;
One drowned,
Then there were four.

Four happy schoolboys saw a bear;
One was scared,
Then there were three.

Three happy schoolboys needed the loo;
One went in,
Then there were two.

Two happy schoolboys fired a gun;
One backfired,
Then there was one.

One happy schoolboy without any fun;
He walked slowly home,
And then there were none.

Michael Willmott (11)
Hayshead Primary School, Arbroath

Ten Happy Schoolboys
(Based on 'Ten Little Schoolboys' by A A Milne)

Ten happy schoolboys standing in a line;
One tripped up and broke his leg,
And then there were nine.

Nine happy schoolboys woke up late;
One went back to sleep,
And then there were eight.

Eight happy schoolboys were standing in Heaven;
One went to Hell,
And then there were seven.

Seven happy schoolboys using some bricks;
One hit himself in the head,
And then there were six.

Six happy schoolboys were trying to dive;
One dived into a shark's mouth,
And then there were five.

Five happy schoolboys went through the door;
One got stuck,
And then there were four.

Four happy schoolboys paying a fee;
One didn't have enough money,
And then there were three.

Three happy schoolboys were drinking, they had a few;
One passed out
And then there were two.

Two happy schoolboys were sitting in the sun;
One got burnt like a burnt pizza,
And then there was one.

One happy schoolboy with no fun;
He walked slowly to school,
And then there were none.

Caitlin Grant (11)
Hayshead Primary School, Arbroath

Ten Happy Schoolgirls
(Based on 'Ten Little Schoolboys' by A A Milne)

Ten happy schoolgirls stood in a line;
One tripped up,
And then there were nine.

Nine happy schoolgirls met at a gate;
One bashed her head,
And then there were eight.

Eight happy schoolgirls went to Devon;
One was carsick,
And then there were seven.

Seven happy schoolgirls playing with bricks;
One broke her toe,
And then there were six.

Six happy schoolgirls trying to jive;
One twisted her ankle,
And then there were five.

Five happy schoolgirls tried to roar;
One girl got a sore throat,
And then there were four.

Four happy schoolgirls swimming in the sea;
One drowned,
And then there were three.

Three happy schoolgirls playing with glue;
One stuck her hands together,
And then there were two.

Two happy schoolgirls playing with a gun;
One shot the other,
And then there was one.

One happy schoolgirl had no fun;
She walked home,
And then there were none.

Sophie Willmott (11)
Hayshead Primary School, Arbroath

Ten Happy Schoolboys
(Based on 'Ten Little Schoolboys' by A A Milne)

Ten happy schoolboys standing in a line,
One got into trouble,
And then there were nine.

Nine happy schoolboys swinging on a gate;
One fell off,
And then there were eight.

Eight happy schoolboys walking to Devon;
One slipped on ice,
And then there were seven.

Seven happy schoolboys playing tricks;
One got caught,
And then there were six.

Six happy schoolboys taking a dive;
One hit a rock,
And then there were five.

Five happy schoolboys jumping on a floor;
One fell through,
And then there were four.

Four happy schoolboys climbing a tree;
One fell down,
And then there were three.

Three happy schoolboys went to the loo;
One didn't come out,
And then there were two.

Two happy schoolboys fired a gun;
One backfired,
And then there was one.

One sad schoolboy with no fun;
Fell off a cliff,
And then there were none.

Denise Buchan (11)
Hayshead Primary School, Arbroath

Ten Happy Schoolboys
(Based on 'Ten Little Schoolboys' by A A Milne)

Ten happy schoolboys drinking wine;
One got a hangover!
And then there were nine.

Nine happy schoolboys climbed a gate;
One fell off,
And then there were eight.

Eight happy schoolboys were joking with Kevin;
One laughed too hard,
And then there were seven.

Seven happy schoolboys were playing tricks;
One went wrong,
And then there were six.

Six happy schoolboys watching TV live;
One shouted too loudly,
And then there were five.

Five happy schoolboys heard a roar;
They saw a lion,
And then there were four.

Four happy schoolboys were in the sea;
The tide came in,
And then there were three.

Three happy schoolboys really needed the loo;
One exploded,
And then there were two.

Two happy schoolboys the lottery they won;
But they got in a fight,
And there was one.

One lonely schoolboy without any fun;
He shot himself down,
And now there were none.

Russell Henderson (11)
Hayshead Primary School, Arbroath

Pink

My sister Ellie's fantastic bedroom,
The bouncy trampoline,
A six can fridge in Mum's bedroom,
A big bang of fireworks,
An attractive perfume,
People shouting and cheering loudly,
The booming of a hooter,
A narrow fraction of spam,
Lots of candyfloss,
Smooth toilet paper,
Gentle silk lamp.

Gavin Cook (11)
Hayshead Primary School, Arbroath

Pink

Bright, lovely fairy room
Smart, cool Timberland boots
VW car that I see in Arbroath
Plug-in air freshener
The beautiful scent of bubble bath
The loud school bell ringing
The sound of my friend's laughter
Jam birthday cake
Strawberry ice cream
A long warm coat
Big, fluffy boots.

Lee Smith (11)
Hayshead Primary School, Arbroath

Pink

Pink looks like . . .
A beautiful, skinny flamingo.
A bright skipping rope.
A cute cuddly, pink teddy bear.

Tastes like . . .
A doughnut with pink icing.
A bottle of strawberry sauce.
And strawberry ice cream.

Sounds like . . .
A band of pink instruments.
Bubbles in champagne.
Beautiful pink fireworks.

Smells like . . .
Pink perfume.
A pink flower.
The icing of a cake.

Feels like . . .
A nice bubble bath.
A fluffy lamp.
A smooth towel.

Dean Smith (11)
Hayshead Primary School, Arbroath

Anger

Anger is purple
It tastes like spicy mustard
And smells like burning tomatoes
It looks like a screwed up face
And sounds like a gun going bang
Anger is when you fall out with your friends.

Shelby Green (10)
Hayshead Primary School, Arbroath

Embarrassment

Embarrassment is green
It tastes like my gran's home-made soup
And smells like burning rubber
It looks like a poisonous mushroom
And sounds like cracked windows
Embarrassment is like life passed.

Natasha Herald (11)
Hayshead Primary School, Arbroath

Sadness

Sadness is light grey
It tastes like cold macaroni
And smells like burning candles
It looks like my mum's steak casserole, yuck!
And is like on my birthday when I miss my dad.

Hannah Harris (11)
Hayshead Primary School, Arbroath

Loneliness

Loneliness is grey
It tastes like cold tea and coffee together
And smells like plain yellow porridge
It looks like a black, dark room
And sounds like a giant's footsteps on your roof
Loneliness is having nowhere to go and nothing to do.

Terri McKenzie (11)
Hayshead Primary School, Arbroath

Scared

Scared is black
It tastes like out of date beans
And smells like old smelly socks
It looks like a scary face
And sounds like a scary monster
Scared is when you are getting into trouble.

Daniel Campbell (11)
Hayshead Primary School, Arbroath

Excitement

Excitement is blue
It tastes like nothing you have tasted before
And smells like lovely, hot baked cakes.
It looks like people full of joy
And sounds like bubbles of the river
Excitement is going on holiday very soon.

Reese Maison (10)
Hayshead Primary School, Arbroath

Loneliness

Loneliness is white
It tastes like out of date bread
And smells like burning buildings
It looks like it is the end of the world
And sounds like World War II
Loneliness is a never-ending tunnel.

Kyle McIntosh (11)
Hayshead Primary School, Arbroath

Anger

Anger is red
It tastes like toxic waste
And smells like hot coal
It looks like a red blob
And sounds like my mum and dad talking
Anger is like a volcano erupting.

Jay Millar (11)
Hayshead Primary School, Arbroath

Frightened

Frightened is brown
It tastes like eggs
And smells like my mum's feet
It looks like a black cloud
And sounds like a scary man laughing
Frightened is being in a scary movie.

Sean Muir (11)
Hayshead Primary School, Arbroath

Sadness

Sadness is dark blue
It tastes like rotting cabbage
And smells of cut garlic
It looks like a dead animal
And sounds like shrill screaming
Sadness is a cold cave with nobody around.

Cameron Ramage (11)
Hayshead Primary School, Arbroath

A Spell To Make All Schools Blow Up
(Based on 'Macbeth')

Round about the cauldron go
Deal in a dead rat's toe
Hurl a hamster's gut in
Chicken's leg found in a bin
Hurl in a human's head
A dead rat's leg found in a bed.

'Double, double, toil and trouble,
Fire burn and cauldron bubble'.

Hurl in a burnt dog's head,
Throw in a broken pig's leg
Beat in a hamster's tail
Put in a bottle of ale.
Then the cauldron will go dark
Only the witch's wand will spark.

'Double double toil and trouble
Fire burn and cauldron bubble'.

Cool it with some monkeys' blood
Then the charm is firm and good.

Daniel Simpson (10)
Hayshead Primary School, Arbroath

Anger

Anger is dark red
It tastes like very hot spices
And smells like Indian mustard
It looks like a dark cloud and sounds like thunder and lightning
Anger makes me grumpy when I have to do something
I don't want to.

John Ryan (10)
Hayshead Primary School, Arbroath

A Spell To Make The School Explode
(Based on 'Macbeth')

Round about the cauldron go
An arrow of blood from a bow
An ant's leg, an egg of a spider
A wing of a fly, a glass of cider
Throw in an alien in the pot
Make it juicy and hot.

'Double double toil and trouble
Fire burn and cauldron bubble'.

Stuff a bat with bones
A goat's tongue, slimy stones.
A cupful of fly's blood
Then a bucketful of worms and mud.

'Double, double toil and trouble
Fire burn and cauldron bubble'.

Round about the cauldron go
Spiders' poison and archer bow
Seagull guts, black cat's brain
A fog eye, a ghost train.
A frog with warts, a pupil's blister
An elephant trunk, then Oliver Twister.

Jason Wood (11)
Hayshead Primary School, Arbroath

Agony

Agony is black and blue
It tastes like a fusty sandwich
And smells like smelly seaweed
It looks like everyone is mad at you
And sounds like a horrible squeaky voice that won't stop
Agony is like pins and needles that won't go away.

Shannon Sinclair (11)
Hayshead Primary School, Arbroath

A Spell To Turn Me Into A Fairy Princess
(Inspired by 'Macbeth')

Round about the cauldron go
Nicely add a sparkly bow,
Strike a pose,
As you carefully add in a bright red rose
Sprinkle in some fairy dust
You better add it quickly before this spell goes bust!

Bubble, bubble we want no trouble
Don't be afraid only nice spells bubble.

Nicely add a pinch of glitter,
But don't put in any litter,
Put in a shining star,
Then meet a princess from afar
Laugh loudly and gently put in the colours of a rainbow
Gently blow in some pearly white snow.

Bubble, bubble, we want no trouble
Don't be afraid - only nice spells bubble.

You better not get in a mood,
Then the charm is firm and good.

Paige Findlay (11)
Hayshead Primary School, Arbroath

Anger

Anger is red
It tastes like chilli peppers
And smells like burning rubber
It looks like hot burning lava
And sounds like a fast zooming rocket
Anger is like an atomic pile driver.

Liam Smith (11)
Hayshead Primary School, Arbroath

A Spell To Make The Teachers And The School Disappear

Round about the cauldron go
Put some skinny legs of a monkey and then throw
Throw in a pig's nose
Dump in broken human toes
Add a fist full of rotten eggs
Stir in some dragon's mouldy legs.

*'Double double toil and trouble
Fire burn and cauldron bubble'.*

Throw in some snake skin
Dump in some rubbish from a bin
Beat in some mice tails
Put in some poisoned ale
Add a fist full of monkey's eyes
Throw in some rotten pies.

*'Double double toil and trouble
Fire burn and cauldron bubble'.*

Cool it down with some human blood
'Then the charm is firm and good'.

John Taylor (11)
Hayshead Primary School, Arbroath

Anger

Anger is grey
It tastes like hot pepper
And it smells like hot, spicy curry.
It looks like a grumpy face
And it sounds like thunder and lightning
Anger is loud and very explosive.

David Teviotdale (12)
Hayshead Primary School, Arbroath

Embarrassment

Embarrassment is red
It tastes like spicy chilli
And smells like hot crisps
It looks like a red face
And sounds like my ears popping
Embarrassment is when I score an own goal.

Stephanie Ward (10)
Hayshead Primary School, Arbroath

Sadness

Sadness is light blue
It tastes like pain
And smells like a cold horrible dungeon
It looks like a person who has a broken heart
And sounds like screaming in your head
Sadness is a crying, painful matter.

John Woodcock (11)
Hayshead Primary School, Arbroath

Happiness

Happiness is pink
It tastes like chips
And smells like the sea
It looks like an ice cream
Happiness is playing a football game.

Luke Waddilove (11)
Hayshead Primary School, Arbroath

Ten Happy Schoolboys
(Based on 'Ten Happy Schoolboys' by A A Milne)

Ten happy schoolboys were playing fine;
One ran off,
And then there were nine.

Nine happy schoolboys were going for a date;
One got left
And then there were eight.

Eight happy schoolboys were going to heaven;
One lost his soul
And then there were seven.

Seven happy schoolboys were eating a Twix;
One ate it too fast
And then there were six.

Six happy schoolboys took a dive;
One couldn't swim
And then there were five.

Five happy schoolboys wanted more;
One wanted it too much
And then there were four.

Four happy schoolboys wanted a cup of tea;
One choked
And then there were three.

Three happy schoolboys wanted to grow;
One shrank
And then there were two.

Two happy schoolboys wanted a piece of gum;
One was not allowed gum
And then there was one.

One sad schoolboy was running home;
He ran too fast
And then there were none.

Jamie Elliott (10)
Hayshead Primary School, Arbroath

Loneliness

Loneliness is blue
Loneliness tastes bittersweet
And smells like mouldy food
It looks like a block of solid ice
And sounds like people running past without seeing you
Loneliness is like being stuck in the desert.

Liam Winton (11)
Hayshead Primary School, Arbroath

Delight

Delight is blue
It tastes like juicy apples just picked
And smells like cinnamon cookies
It looks like a baby smiling
And sounds like laughter from everyone
Delight is a happy way of life.

Lori Cargill (11)
Hayshead Primary School, Arbroath

Cyril The Squirrel

There is an animal in our garden
And I call him Cyril.
He ran up the walnut tree
I shouted, 'Hi Cyril the squirrel.'
Cyril is sneaky, he jumps and he's sly
Goes from branch to branch high up in the sky.
Knocks down some walnuts,
Munch, munch, munch,
'Hmm I'll have these for my lunch.'

Rachel Mottershead (9)
Ysgol Gynradd Bronington, Whitchurch

The Magic Box
(Based on 'Magic Box' by Kit Wright)

I will put in the box . . .
Fireworks flying,
Rainbows bursting into flames,
Chestnuts roasting, marshmallows melting.

I will put in the box . . .
The smiling moon in the jewel-strewn sky,
The fiery orange sun and candyfloss clouds,
And all the twittering birds too.

I will put in the box . . .
The warm, golden yellow sand,
The waves of the sapphire blue sea lapping,
And the soft blowing wind.

My box is fashioned from sparkling crystals and fire flames,
With gemstones on the lid and memories in the corners.
The hinges are made from the splinters from a camel's tail.

Abigail Fawcett, Heather Davies & Ellie Ryder (10)
Ysgol Gynradd Bronington, Whitchurch

The Magic Box
(Based on 'Magic Box' by Kit Wright)

I will put in the box . . .
The swish of a silk scarf on a winter morning
Smoke from the mouth of the Welsh dragon
The jagged dragon's finger of Snowdonia.

I will put in the box . . .
A snowman with a shivering carrot
A sip of the clearest icy water from Bale Lake
The leap of a trout in the boiling rapids of the Dee.

My box is fashioned from slate as black as coal
From the deepest mines in Wales.
It is covered with the dragon's scales.
Its hinges are the claws of the dragon.

Richard Jones (10)
Ysgol Gynradd Bronington, Whitchurch

The Magic Box
(Based on 'Magic Box' by Kit Wright)

I will put in the box . . .
The swish of falling snow on a winter night,
Ice from the nostrils of a winter dragon,
The tip of a tongue touching the ice-cold teeth.

I will put in the box . . .
A snowman melting in the burning hot sun,
The water from the coral sea shimmering in the heat,
A flame leaping off an electric fish.

I will put in the box . . .
Three black wishes spoken in Gujarati,
The last curse of an ancient crone
And the cry of a lost soul.

My box is fashioned from sparkling crystals and fire flames
With gemstones on the lid and memories in the corners.
Its hinges are made from the claws of an old hag.

Sam Evans (10) & Michael Roberts
Ysgol Gynradd Bronington, Whitchurch

The Magic Box
(Based on 'Magic Box' by Kit Wright)

I will put in the box . . .
The swish of a silk scarf on a winter morning,
Smoke from the nostrils of a Welsh dragon,
The tip of a finger touching a tooth.

I will put in the box . . .
A snowman with a carrot nose,
A sip of sapphire water from Lake Bala,
A lightning flash of a salmon in the Dee.

My box is made of frost from Mount Snowdon,
It's wrapped up by a tear off the Welsh flag.

Jacob Kendall (9)
Ysgol Gynradd Bronington, Whitchurch

The Magic Box
(Based on 'Magic Box' by Kit Wright)

I will put in the box . . .
The swish of a silky scarf on a winter morning,
Snow from the nostrils of an ice dragon,
The tip of a tongue touching an ice cream.

I will put in the box . . .
A snowman melting on a hot day,
A gulp of the icy water from Bala Lake,
Water droplets dripping from a fish on a fisherman's line.

I will put in the box . . .
An ice age with a beaming sun,
A snowman on a broomstick,
A witch with stick arms.

My box is fashioned from sparkling crystals and flames from a burning fire,
With gemstones on the lid and memories in the corners,
The hinges are the toe joints of our ancient ancestors.

Bethany Loveridge (11) & Joshua Bailey (10)
Ysgol Gynradd Bronington, Whitchurch

Horses

Some horses are red, some are white
Some horses are dull, some are bright
Some horses say nothing and some sing
Some horses plod, some have a spring
Some horses run and some jump
Some horses have lots of rosettes,
Some none.

Sammy O'Brien (9)
Ysgol Gynradd Bronington, Whitchurch